BUILDING AND OPERATING
A REALISTIC MODEL RAILWAY

A GUIDE TO RUNNING A LAYOUT LIKE AN ACTUAL RAILWAY

BUILDING AND OPERATING
A REALISTIC MODEL RAILWAY

A GUIDE TO RUNNING A LAYOUT LIKE AN ACTUAL RAILWAY

Allen Jackson

THE CROWOOD PRESS

First published in 2016 by
The Crowood Press Ltd
Ramsbury, Marlborough
Wiltshire SN8 2HR

www.crowood.com

British Library Cataloguing-in-Publication Data
A catalogue record for this book is available from the British Library.

ISBN 978 1 78500 169 7

Dedication
For Ninette.

Acknowledgements
To signallers and other railway staff who have been kind enough to share their
interest and experiences with me.

Author's note
I have tried to make this book eminently practical as well as perhaps readable. Not
only that, there is some idea of what it will cost if you decide to build something
yourself; these prices were accurate at the time of writing (September 2015).

Disclaimer
The author and the publisher do not accept any responsibility in any manner
whatsoever for any error or omission, or any loss, damage, injury, adverse outcome,
or liability of any kind incurred as a result of the use of any of the information
contained in this book, or reliance upon it. If in doubt about any aspect of railway
modelling readers are advised to seek professional advice.

Frontispiece
Fig. 1   Northern Rail class 153 is about to depart from Platform 2 at Dovedale station
and take the left-hand branch at the tunnel mouth to Buxton. The two semaphore
signals indicate the points are correctly set, as they are interlocked, and the colour
light indicates that track power is selected to the Dovedale operator so that the train
can be driven straight into the fiddle yard.

Typeset by Jean Cussons Typesetting, Diss, Norfolk
Printed and bound in Malaysia by Times Offset (M) Sdn Bhd

CONTENTS

INTRODUCTION

The initial thrill of operating a new train-set eventually fades and perhaps you get round to thinking 'Is this all there is?'; and whilst a train set provides the basics of a train that moves, there are so many aspects to real railway operation that provide a fascinating and satisfying continuation of the hobby to provide an enduring appeal.

The emphasis on prototype railway operation has built up over the years to be one of control and safety. In the early days, some horrific accidents gradually changed the operating ethos from one that involved elements of chance, where passengers' lives took a turn on the roulette wheel, to a network based on efficiency and safety.

The media are never slow to tell us of overcrowding and delays due to over-running engineering works but the railway is suffering growing pains again after fifty years of being rundown and neglected. Real substantial efforts are being made at all levels to build and run railways that the nation can be proud of. You only have to look at the recent television documentaries about First Great Western and East Coast Trains, where the staff have contracted that peculiarly un-British condition of unswerving customer service, to realize the sea change that has been going on. Let's hope it's highly infectious.

You may take it from this that the book will be about a model railway that is bang up to date and reflects Network Rail and the train-operating companies as they were when this book was written in 2015. That said, the railways are a mixture of the most modern and Victorian infrastructures side by side, and therein lies a part of the fascination with the current railway scene. It is a scene that is rapidly changing and a way of life that is disappearing.

Also, to have written a book about building a model railway in the steam age would probably not appeal to those setting off on model railway building as, preserved railways apart, it is now so long ago as to be beyond the memory or experience of all but bus-pass holders.

The building of a model railway is something that requires an holistic approach or one that involves the whole process to achieve realism. Early on in the planning for this book it was decided to build a model railway layout from scratch specifically in support of the book, and to invite the readers along for the ride and even have a go. In this mostly post-industrial society fewer people are constructing or making things for themselves in their work and yet the feeling abroad is that many would like to do so as a hobby. This book assumes little prior knowledge other than that you may know one end of a screwdriver from the other, but not necessarily what kind of a screwdriver it is.

The building of a model railway layout needs many skills and a few might include: woodworking, technical drawing, electrician, civil engineering, model craft, metalworking and painter. It is highly unlikely that everyone embarking on this project will have all the skills, but they can all be acquired to the degree necessary; the one quality needed is persistence. The nature of this particular beast is that folk will be doing stuff they haven't done before and that is always a little daunting, but persistence always pays off. You will get there eventually. There are always dodges and shortcuts that can be employed as a substitute for skill in a particular department, and the book makes full use of them.

Costs are seemingly an unanswered question in books like this and it may be the one thing that can put people off if they don't know how much to budget for. The layout as built is fully costed – except where it comes down to rolling stock, which is very personal and depends on whether it was bought new or second-hand. In any case, this is one area where Google can assist with the information.

The costs will be for the layout built and that will not apply directly to everyone, but a ball-park figure will be arrived at and clearly the costs can be incurred over time as the layout is built.

Also not directly costed in are tools, as these costs would be amortized or spread out over the life of such items, which should be years, but some indications of costs of tools appear.

A mixture of imperial and metric units appear in the book as that commonly reflects society as it currently is but, where appropriate, the other equivalent of the units used will be quoted.

Fig. 2 Freightliner class 66 has run round its train of limestone wagons and is now signalled for Buxton and Manchester.

CHAPTER ONE

LAYOUT PLANNING

SCALE AND GAUGE

The railway featured in this book was built to OO gauge – rolling stock for which is in 4mm to the foot scale – and it might be helpful to define the difference between what we mean by scale and by gauge as this will help us make an early planning decision.

Scale is the ratio of the model to the real thing and can be expressed as, for example:

1:76 scale – in other words, the model is $\frac{1}{76}$th the size of the real thing.

This value is often quoted on model road vehicles and buildings to let us know they would be suitable for the layout.

OO gauge refers to the distance between the rails of the model. There is no such thing as OO scale.

The top part of the not-to-scale diagram (Fig. 3) shows an end-on view of a piece of track and the track gauge of 16.5mm, which is OO gauge. Using our 4mm to the foot scale, we can see that the track gauge of 16.5mm divided by 4mm is equal to a track gauge of 4ft 6in in real life, which is too narrow for an absolute scale model.

The standard gauge in Britain and 60 per cent of the rest of the world is 4ft 8½in or 1,435mm. It is sometimes called the Stephenson Gauge after George Stephenson, a railway pioneer.

HO gauge – which also has a 16.5mm track gauge – is 3.5mm to the foot and so the outline of the rolling stock would be smaller if British outline rolling stock were used, but it is mainly found on the European continental scene. The European loading gauge or size of rolling stock allowed to go through tunnels and bridges is considerably larger than in Britain. The Channel Tunnel accommodates the larger con-

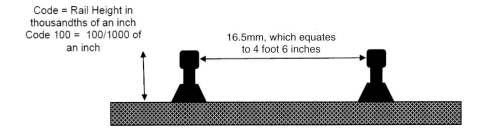

Code = Rail Height in thousandths of an inch
Code 100 = 100/1000 of an inch

16.5mm, which equates to 4 foot 6 inches

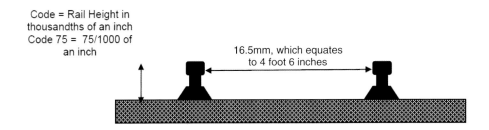

Code = Rail Height in thousandths of an inch
Code 75 = 75/1000 of an inch

16.5mm, which equates to 4 foot 6 inches

*Fig. 3
Schematic diagram of track gauges and rail heights in OO gauge.*

tinental rolling stock, as well as special vehicles to carry trucks and cars, but Eurostar trains conform to the smaller British loading gauge.

There is an organization called the EM Gauge Society (where EM means Eighteen Millimetres) who model to a track gauge of 18.2mm, and there is even the Protofour or P4 Association who model to an absolute track gauge of 18.83mm. These two, plus OO gauge modellers, all still model to 4mm to the foot scale.

The trouble is that none of the locomotives or rolling stock you can buy in the shops will run on the broader gauges, and to convert your favourite class 66 to run on EM, for example, would need specialist wheel sets from Ultrascale, adding over £50 to the cost of the one locomotive.

There is a dodge whereby the track gauge can look tolerably close to scale standards and a lot better than the usual but still use track you can buy in the shops and trains likewise. This has to do with

an early planning decision that was taken for this book – the layout was to be a secondary line not the East or West Coast Main Lines. Most bedrooms or other domestic accommodation will not be suited to modelling the iconic quadruple track main line from Euston to Watford, for example.

Figure 4 shows the main line and siding at Thetford in Norfolk. The main line is modern-ish flat-bottomed rail, soon to be replaced, and the siding bull-head rail. The difference in rail height shows up well here.

Flat-bottomed rail was introduced as a more stable rail capable of taking heavier loads at higher speeds, and per unit length it weighs considerably more than bull head. The other advantage of flat-bottomed is that it can use metal clips to attach the rail to the sleepers instead of chairs and wooden blocks or steel springs, which have to be hand-assembled with bull-head railed track. Flat-bottom railed track can be factory made in sections.

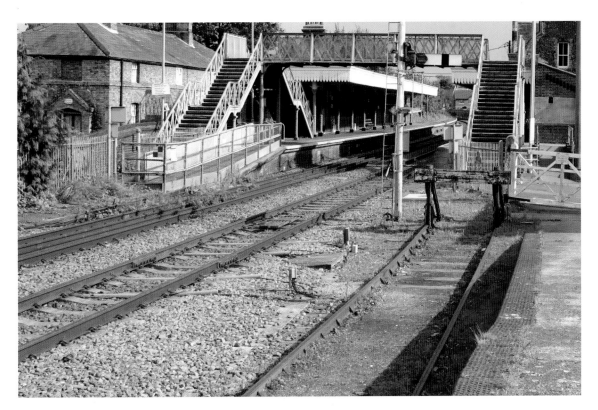

Fig. 4   Comparison of flat-bottomed and bull-head rail heights, Thetford, Norfolk.

Fig. 5 White-painted rail at March South Junction crossing, Cambridgeshire.

However, because of cost and the sheer scale of the task, many secondary lines continue to use bull-head rail where speeds, in particular with freight trains, on secondary lines are not high.

Back to Fig. 3 and it can be seen that the track gauge of the lower, bull-head rail piece of track appears to be of wider gauge, although it is identical to the top section of track.

Choosing code 75 railed track on a secondary lined model of a prototype is fine on both counts of scale appearance and fidelity to the prototype. Code 75 it is then. Any type of rail can have its appearance improved by painting the rails rust coloured, which they nearly all are in real life, and this too has the visual effect of lowering the rail height and thereby making the track gauge look true to the prototype gauge. Code 100 rail was originally used by model railway manufacturers, as they were using wheels with large flanges, known as coarse scale. The rail needed to be higher up to avoid the flanges hitting the sleepers. There are no popular manufacturers of locomotives and rolling stock in 4mm scale that use coarse scale any longer.

Some rails on the prototype are painted white, which, in the context of track gauge perception, makes the rails look taller and the track gauge narrower.

Figure 5 amply illustrates the point and was taken in April 2015 at March South Junction in Cambridgeshire. The rails are painted white here because the track under the crossing is considered to be under additional stress to plain track. This stress, plus the heat of a sunny day, can cause cracks in the rail with potentially fatal consequences. Painting the rails white lowers the surface temperature by up to 2°C (3.6°F). Even this early in the year, the track gang was out measuring the rail temperature and they told me that the temperature was 31°C (87.8°F). The temperature limit before Network Rail start reducing the speed of the trains is 33°C (91.4°F).

LAYOUT TYPE

There are basically two types of layout in popular use and they are continuous run and end to end.

With the exception of the Circle Line on the London Underground, and the Docklands Light

Railway, all railways run from point A to B and then possibly C and branch off for D and so on.

The concept of the end-to-end layout is of a train carrying out a journey and, although most of us are constrained by money and space to only model the last part of a journey, the continuous run nearly always takes up a good deal more room and does not operate like a real railway.

These thoughts are constrained by the desire to run trains as the prototype runs them. If all you want is a test track to run trains round there is nothing wrong in that but that is not what this book is about.

In other words, this book is about building a model of a prototype railway, insofar as that is possible within space constraints. Although the location will be imaginary, there have to be enough prototypical features to make the railway a believable, real location, and the way it works has to reflect what is done on the real thing. I say the location is imaginary and that is because it is virtually impossible to model to scale any prototype exactly – they

are just too big. The largest size of layout that would fit the space I have available is 12ft by 2ft (3.66m by 0.61m). This means two boards of 6ft by 2ft (1.83m by 0.61m). As this is the most convenient and economical size for wood to be purchased, and also as what leaves the fiddle yard will be the same length as what arrives at the station. It will mean that the station and fiddle yard, or the part of the layout that represents the rest of the railway system, will be accommodated on one board each, pretty much.

PROTOTYPE SCENARIO

A specific prototype that would fit the model exists at Buxton in Derbyshire and it consists of two freight lines that meet in a junction. Freight trains run into an interchange siding, the locomotive runs round and the train then departs to a different destination that is in parallel with the original.

Figure 6 explains this a little better. The class 66 and mineral train have emerged from private sidings, which are a branch off the main line. The

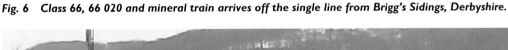

Fig. 6   Class 66, 66 020 and mineral train arrives off the single line from Brigg's Sidings, Derbyshire.

Fig. 7 Peak Forest South looking towards Great Rocks Junction, Derbyshire.

train is about to take the crossover in the foreground and this leads to a long loop. The loco then runs round its train and then departs, taking the tracks we can see to the left of the signal box. These tracks lead to the rest of the rail system at Chinley Junction. The snow will not be modelled. This could mean two tracks from the fiddle yard leading to a loop line and siding for cripple wagons and possibly a locomotive stabling point. The tracks in Fig. 6 past the signal box to the extreme right of the picture lead to Buxton Station, so it is proposed to run Northern Rail DMU trains into a simplified station platform from the fiddle yard. There are actually very few places in the country where shunting and running round of freight trains takes place in Britain, and Derbyshire, centred around Peak Forest, Great Rocks Junction and Buxton, is one of the few and the busiest.

Figure 7 is at Peak Forest South with class 66 on the left shunting a train of limestone wagons, class 60 in the sidings with crippled wagons and a further class 66 on the right at the DB Schenker locomotive stabling point. The depot looks as though it carries out basic inspections and refuelling. The

freight trains from Buxton, referred to in Fig. 6, arrive here travelling towards the camera. From the single-track branch at Buxton the line now has double running tracks, which are to the left of the signal box. The arrangement of the tracks is like the roads in Britain where the railways also 'drive on the left', so to speak. Most continental railways 'drive on the right' as per their roads. The semaphore signalling reflects this and the signals are usually placed to the left of the track they refer to, but this can change. Of paramount importance is the early view the driver gets of any signal and to this end signals are placed where they can be seen the best.

Clearly this could not all be modelled in the space we have but some of the flavour can be captured.

TRACK LAYOUT DIAGRAM

The not-to-scale schematic diagram at Fig. 8 is an initial view of what the facilities would be before the layout is built and before accurate sizing on the actual boards has taken place.

In every project engineering department, one activity invariably taking place is the production

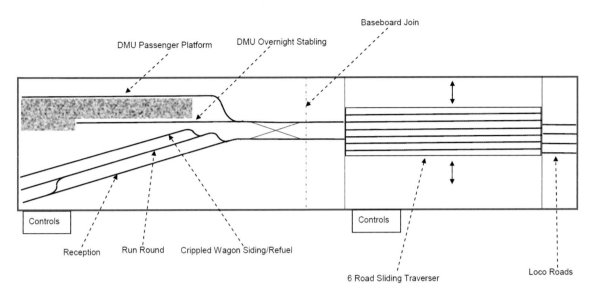

Fig. 8 Initial layout track diagram and arrangement of baseboards.

of 'as built' drawings. In other words, things can change and the finished product may vary from the initial design for all sorts of reasons.

Some design notes on the diagram:

Starting at the baseboard join and travelling to the left is a scissors' crossover, which enables either of the two single-track lines coming out of the fiddle yard to access either the freight or passenger facilities. This represents the two single lines we saw at Buxton in Fig. 6 but they have both been enabled to carry passenger trains, which neither of the Buxton branches do, although passenger trains do access a station nearby but not via the branches.

This is a 'scissors crossover', which consists of four points and a diamond crossing, but in the model will be a double-slip, basically the same facilities but compressed to save space and, in addition, it only needs two point motors instead of four.

In Fig. 9, the double-slip is the piece of track with four tracks leading into it between the two sets of Lafarge wagons. It acts as a scissors' crossover

but is only used in slow-speed areas like station approaches and such like.

The freight tracks lead off to the bottom left-hand corner of the diagram, nearest the station controls, and it is here that most uncoupling will need to be done and so it is closest to the operator. The passenger facilities, on the other hand, shouldn't need uncoupling facilities at all and can be kept at the opposite side to the operator.

The freight roads are canted at an angle and this is to accommodate the maximum length of train possible.

The fiddle yard uses a traverser – a sliding bridge on rails used to transfer locos and rolling stock between tracks without the need for points (see http://wikimapia.org/18765725/Traverser). This allows the maximum train length possible in the baseboard length we have. If points were to be employed, most of the space would be taken up by the points themselves and the resultant sidings would be woefully inadequate as regards wagon capacity. The 1ft or 305mm run in and run off to the traverser allows locos to run round trains and there can be a multitude of other sidings in parallel to the run off and run on traverser roads. The

Fig. 9 Double-slip pictured between the LaFarge wagons at Earl's Sidings, Derbyshire.

traverser is 4ft long (1,220mm) and this compares very well with the reception siding length.

Each traverser road has a push-button dead section at the end, which enables a train to be run from the station area and to come to an automatic halt, handy if operating on your own.

The traverser road furthest away from the fiddle yard operator is reserved for DMU traffic, once again because of the no-coupling requirement. The next road would be a run round to enable locomo-

---

DISCLAIMER

In the construction phases that follow some companies are named and their products put forward and this is purely as a result of experiences with such outfits in the past. There is no commercial link between any such company and the author or publisher.

---

tives to head up trains. The other four roads nearest the fiddle yard operator are for freight traffic. This will get mixed up in the hurly burly of operating but these are what is required.

TRACK MANUFACTURERS

The decision has been made to go with code 75 rail, as that will give the most prototypical appearance for the type of line being built. There are several track options and perhaps an overview of them will not come amiss.

SMP (Scale Model Products) – Marcway – is based on the purchase of single rails to which is soldered cut-up, printed circuit-board strips for sleepers. A jig has to be manufactured and curved track has to be constructed in situ, as the finished item is rigid. The only way to undo this is to unsolder. After the track has been assembled, it has to be cut to ensure there are no short-circuits. Then the track has to be cleaned off from the soldering process, primed and sprayed with sleeper colour black/brown. Then the rails need to be painted rusty brown and the surfaces wiped off. The track is then ready to lay. It is highly realistic, runs well, is easy to make adjustments and much cheaper than factory-made track, but large amounts of work are needed to make the jigs and then the track, so this may not be suitable if you are just starting out.

C&L Finescale is a similar concept to above except that chairs are glued to sleepers and rails affixed to chairs. Great care is needed and there is much work required to get the track to operate reliably. Plywood sleepers have holes drilled in them to which is attached a copper or similar rivet. The rail is soldered to the rivet using track gauges and cosmetic chairs, and detail is glued on afterwards. It looks the business but it is highly labour-intensive.

Peco Streamline needs the minimum of effort to get it to work and with some subtle modifications can look quite realistic.

The decision was made to go for Peco Streamline as it was felt that newcomers would be more comfortable with the choice and be able to cope and see something for their efforts in a reasonable timescale.

EXHIBITION MATTERS OR PORTABILITY

It may seem premature to involve this in our planning but this is one area that needs to be addressed at this stage because, if you do decide to exhibit the layout, retrospective action to make it portable will involve much more work than if it is catered for now.

The largest single issue is that the baseboards can be divided into two, as they most certainly will not be going anywhere if they remain in 12ft by 2ft (3.66m by 0.61m) format. There are other issues, such as moving home or if you sell the layout, so it will need to be portable.

It may also seem odd that this is being discussed about what may be your first layout but if the smell of the crowd and the roar of the greasepaint appeals to you there is no barrier. The main thing is that, apart from the railway looking presentable, it must operate properly and to a recognized sequence that ensures that something is moving all the time. This is not easy on an end-to-end layout but will endear you to exhibition managers and the paying public. There are so many exhibition layouts that either don't work properly or there is no organization to a sequence, and so movement is restricted to spasmodic events, where the public gets fed up waiting for something to happen and wanders off. Continuous run layouts are not immune from this condition either and have less of an excuse.

Writing a sequence for this model railway is one of the chapters and a sequence adds immeasurably to the fun you get operating the layout because this is what real railways do, only they call it a working timetable.

If the baseboards divide, then so must the wiring, and multi-way plugs and sockets will need to be plumbed in between boards and control panels. In addition, you may wish to insert another board at some point, and so the boards must be divisible from that standpoint.

There are many other issues yet to be addressed, such as signalling, ways of working and other prototypical features, which will form some of the succeeding chapters of the book. For now though, there is enough planning done to start work building it.

PROJECT MANAGEMENT

This layout building is undoubtedly a project and it needs management. We have all seen projects where possibly the management input was insufficient – Wembley Stadium, Millennium Bridge, Edinburgh Tram system and so forth. With anything that has Millennium in the title, clearly an end date is crucial, and we are all grateful the 2012 Olympics happened in 2012!

With a hobby, time and date are not as crucial, unless you are building to an exhibition deadline. Costs are the main issue here and so some monitoring and control of costs will ensure that the layout remains affordable. A summary of layout costs will be found in Appendix I.

CHAPTER TWO

LAYOUT CONSTRUCTION

BASEBOARD CONSTRUCTION

There are to be two 6ft (1,420mm) by 2ft (610mm) baseboards and as there is a high degree of track present, a solid baseboard top was chosen.

Another option is where a branch line runs through countryside in, say, a cutting, when it can be advantageous to lay a track bed and then surround the track bed with formers to make construction of the cutting easier and more realistic.

As to materials, the current vogue is 75mm by 25mm (3 by 1in) planed timber made into a frame and topped with 9mm ply for the track and scenery surface. This costs about three times as much as the solution chosen here and delivers no tangible benefits. If, after railway use, you require the baseboards to be a model of a World War II Vosper Thorneycroft RAF Air Sea Rescue Launch or possibly a Pathfinder RAF Mosquito, then go with plywood, otherwise save your money. The main requirement is that a baseboard must be capable of taking and holding a small woodscrew.

All of the initial baseboard material was purchased from B&Q and whilst they are not the cheapest for everything, they are nationwide and so someone reading this in Inverness, Pembroke Dock, Ballymena, Chichester or Lowestoft, or anywhere in between, could acquire these items. Also, if you buy too much of any one item, they take it back provided it is as bought. However, there will be some screws left over from the 1,000 in the box but they are not returnable.

Figure 10 shows the shopping list above, as bought. The rough-sawn timber can be smoothed down with sandpaper but most of it will remain covered up and so this is not necessary. The layout sides will be finished off with hardboard and so most of the rough-sawn timber will be obscured from view.

Figure 11 has the basic tools needed to start the process and others will be needed as work progresses. The grey mains-powered item is a mitre saw, which is needed to cut pieces of the 1,800mm rough-sawn timber accurately and at right angles to length to form the framework. The alternative is to use a set square to accurately mark out the timber and saw around the mark. If your sawing is not that accurate, it will show. The mitre saw was about £20 and is the 'cheapo' version, but we are

Material Costs: Baseboard Construction

Item Description	Quantity	Cost each – 2015	Sub-Total
1,828 × 610 × 12mm Chipboard	2	£11.08	£22.16
1,800 × 38 × 25mm rough-sawn timber	Pack of 8 timbers ×3	£8.00	£24.00
Drywall 40mm countersunk Philips head screws	Pack of 1,000 in 1 box	£7.00	£7.00
Total Cost			**£53.16**

ABOVE: **Fig. 10 Basic baseboard materials.**

not cabinet-makers to the Royal Court of Louis XIV or any other mark of Louis come to that – it will do the job. The drill bit in the power drill is 3mm in size and will be used to drill a pilot hole to guide the screws in. The screwdriver bit in the smaller power drill is a posidrive, cross-pointed or Phillips-type bit.

STATION BASEBOARD

The not-to-scale diagram at Fig. 12 shows exactly how the main 72in (1,828mm) rough-sawn timbers form nearly all the length of a long side and another piece of the rough-sawn timber makes up that long side. In other words, we only need one saw cut to do three sides of the frame. The rest of the frame is made up by cutting five pieces of rough-sawn timber to the dimensions shown.

The 2ft or (610mm) of the long lengths of rough sawn timber can be marked for cutting by placing against the edge of the chipboard and marking with a felt-tip pen and then cutting with the mitre saw. Make sure that the blade of the mitre saw is right on the line by lowering the blade first with no power on. Then, fingers out of the way, make the cut. I say this because a saw cut will be of a certain width and may affect the length of cut if you are not careful.

Fig. 11 The basic tools used to construct the baseboards.

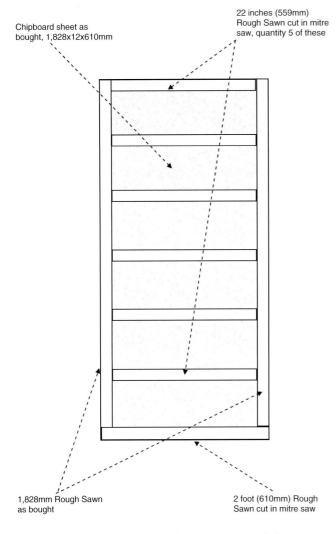

Chipboard sheet as bought, 1,828x12x610mm

22 inches (559mm) Rough Sawn cut in mitre saw, quantity 5 of these

1,828mm Rough Sawn as bought

2 foot (610mm) Rough Sawn cut in mitre saw

Fig. 12   Overview diagram of the construction of the station baseboard.

There may have to be a few pieces of wood expended in the quest for satisfactory results but this is quite normal when you are starting off.

So we now have the five pieces of 22in (559mm), one piece of 24in (610mm) and the two as bought 72in (1,828mm) plus a chipboard sheet. Before we can assemble the frame to the chipboard, we need to mark out the chipboard so that we have a good idea that the screws will be going into the frame timbers.

Use a piece of the rough-sawn timber as a guide to mark out the chipboard prior to drilling and affixing the frame (Fig. 13). The chipboard will rest on the narrow 1in (25mm) edge of the rough-sawn timber, so use this edge down on the chipboard to mark out the edge within which the screws must be if they are to go through the chipboard and into the rough-sawn timber frame.

After the pilot hole has been drilled more or less in the middle of the marked-out line, we can countersink or recess the hole to take the screw head (Fig. 14). This is vital for the smooth running of the trains, as some of the track will be laid across the top of the screw heads and, therefore, there must be no suggestion of a screwhead protruding above the surface. The countersink tool is shown fitted to a

Fig. 13   Marking out a chipboard sheet ready to have the frame screwed to it.

Fig. 14   A baseboard has its frame secured to the rough-sawn timbers and the screws countersunk.

Fig. 15   Showing the use of a square to mark off the place where pilot holes will be drilled on the chipboard to attach the framing.

manual handbrace, as all you need is a few turns to make the recess.

Should you get fed-up with this after a while, the electric screwdriver with the Phillips screwdriver bit makes an admirable countersinker with just a quick burst. You could only really do this with chipboard and certainly not with any metal.

One thing to note, when you are putting in screws in the rough-sawn timber ends, as opposed to the chipboard, remember that the two pieces of rough sawn are only 24mm thick in total and therefore need a shallower pilot hole, say 15mm.

The intermediate 22in (559mm) bracing struts are now fitted. Mark the rough-sawn timber edge pieces along their length at 12in (305mm) intervals and position the crosspieces as shown in Fig. 15. They should be a tap-into-place fit. Mark up using a square, as shown, with a felt-tip pen on both sides of the board. Join the two sets of mark-ups such that you have a crosswise pair of lines within which you can drill pilot holes that will take screws to go through and hold the chipboard to the cross-strut.

Figure 16 shows the intended effect of the previous procedure and demonstrates that the line drawing and so forth were necessary, as you cannot see the cross-struts underneath.

Fig. 16   The purpose of the marking out in Fig. 15 is clearer, as the supporting piece of rough-sawn timber cannot be seen but we still need to secure it to chipboard.

Fig. 17 The piece of end framing for the next board is clamped to the now built baseboard.

Note how the line of screws stops short of the ends, as this is where the side pieces are screwed into the cross-struts and we would not wish the two to collide. Note how smooth and well-finished the timber is – why pay more?

It does not require the centre of the line to be marked out, that is just a guess but works fine. There is no prescription as to how many screws will be needed but as the box contains 1,000, we can be generous and there will still be plenty left for future work.

Before the station board is finished, the next job is to prepare one end to connect to the fiddle yard board. First of all cut another piece of 24in (610mm) rough-sawn timber; this is to be the piece of the fiddle yard board frame that marries up to the now existing station board. Mark out the place where this is to be drilled – 6in (150mm) from the ends and in the centre of the 38mm-wide piece of rough-sawn timber.

As shown in Fig. 17, clamp the piece just marked out to the end of the station board so that the rough-sawn timbers exactly line up. You can use a G-clamp, as shown, or a large pair of Mole grips; failing that you could screw the two pieces together with two 40mm screws, perhaps with some help. Then drill the pre-marked spots with an 8mm drill bit and try to keep the drill at right angles to the wood surface.

Not available from B&Q and in fact only available from Red Dog Models (9 Harcourt Bradwell, Milton Keynes MK13 9EN), as far as is known, are the baseboard joiners.

Figure 18 depicts one set of baseboard joiners: one of the 'screw' pieces has a thread and the other does not. The two 'screw' parts of the joiners have four teeth, which are uppermost in the picture, and

Fig. 18 Red Dog baseboard joiners. Note the fixing on the left is threaded but the one on the right is not.

these bite into either side of the baseboard end-pieces into which we have drilled 8mm holes.

The 8mm bolt with the hexagon head slides into one board end, which has no screw thread, and screws into the next. When the bolt is tightened up it draws the two end-pieces together and hence clamps the boards together and in the right position because we clamped them up that way before drilling the holes. This is all the board-to-board mechanical kit you should need. There are brass pins that locate into brass sockets but they still have to be accurately fitted and positioned; I have never found them to be necessary. You could even just use coach bolts and nuts with a large penny washer underneath the nut to make sure you do not crush the wood. It works but will wear with time and the 8mm holes you drilled will become larger and the baseboards will not quite line up any more, so you will have to put them into position by hand.

Baseboard joiners represent an investment of about £5 but Red Dog do not have a website, so you will have to write a letter to them for their current price list. They advertise in the *Railway Modeller* magazine, so it might be wise to check there first. Red Dog are fairly typical of some of the cottage industries that support model railway construction, but typically give good customer service and you get the personal touch.

Figure 19 show the baseboard ends' joining process. The station board is on the left and the end-piece for the fiddle yard board is still clamped to the station board end-piece framing. As the bolt is tightened, it draws the non-screw threaded piece next to the bolt head and the screw threaded piece in the station end-board together. The two 'screw' pieces will then be permanently in position and the two ends will subsequently line up after being taken apart. The ratchet handle and socket, which is marked ½in, makes the process much quicker.

Please note: no metric conversion is given here as there is no socket manufactured that is a direct fit size-wise for ½in. The nearest metric socket that would fit would be 13mm. The socket sets quoted have both metric and imperial units sockets.

A socket set is available on eBay for under £10, including delivery, and is suitable for use on model railways. Should you subsequently acquire a Ferrari 246 Dino with the V6 engine and you need to remove the cylinder head bolts, you will need to spend more on a socket set. In other words, the light nature of the engineering involved does not warrant large sums being spent on tools when it is not necessary, but if you are intending to use the tools elsewhere, then spend more.

The final task of the preparation of the fiddle yard board end is to mark it up as such. It will only fit –

Fig. 19
Demonstrates the use of a socket and ratchet handle to clamp up the two baseboard ends.

Fig. 20 Two framing ends bolted together.

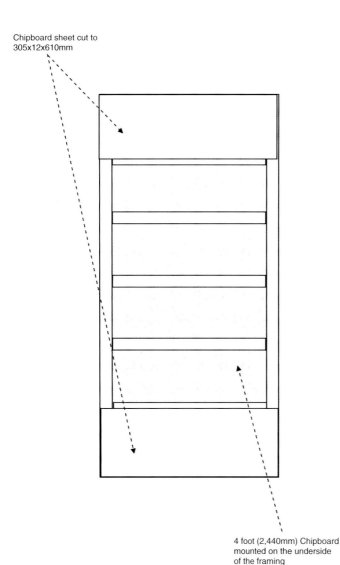

Chipboard sheet cut to 305x12x610mm

4 foot (2,440mm) Chipboard mounted on the underside of the framing

Fig. 21 Overview of the construction of the fiddle yard baseboard.

and line the boards up – one way (Fig. 20). The 8mm-diameter coach bolts were just a preliminary fitting to make sure it lined up before putting the Red Dog kit in place.

No track is laid at this stage, until both boards are fitted together. The track will be laid across both boards, where needed, and then cut in situ after it has been secured and ballasted.

FIDDLE YARD BASEBOARD

The basic framework of the fiddle yard board is the same as the one that we've just made, only this time we have the readymade end for the frame that will couple up with the station baseboard. Make sure that the piece is on the inside of the frame and the right way up, as per the felt-tip pen markings in Fig. 20.

You can still use the second chipboard piece as bought as a template to lay the timbers on before you screw them to each other first. The chipboard securing comes afterwards.

Figure 21 gives a plan or overview of the fiddle yard board. After the framework is finished, we can make two cuts in the chipboard, from either ends of 1ft (305mm). These two pieces form the run on from the station and run off from the traverser. The remaining 4ft (1,219mm) of chipboard is affixed to the underside of the framing and this

Fig. 22 Station baseboard largely complete.

gives extra rigidity to the structure and also forms a safety net if an item of rolling stock should fall off the sliding traverser deck.

Figure 22 is the completed fiddle yard framework prior to securing the chipboard pieces. The felt-tip pen lettering is the indicator as to which side is up and where the chipboard will be secured.

Figure 23 shows the completed fiddle yard board parked on top of the station board, as it is as yet legless.

Fig. 23 The fiddle yard baseboard is complete except for the sliding traverser deck.

LAYOUT LEGS

I had originally thought of building my own trestle table-type legs but common sense prevailed over my limited woodworking skills and for once I decided to splash the cash. However, caution was not thrown entirely to the winds as these items cost not much more than wooden ones to build. They cost £90 for four delivered from eBay but I noticed almost identical ones for sale subsequently for £35 a pair delivered.

The layout legs on show are supposed to be for builders or DIY enthusiasts to suspend builder's planks between for working at altitude. They have a load capacity of 150kg (330lb) each. The additional attraction is that they stow when transported and are of variable height. They can be raised such that a person working underneath the boards could sit

Fig. 24   One of the builder's trestles needed to support the layout.

on a chair whilst doing so – a considerable comfort and a back-saver. Alternatively, the assumption is made that the operators will stand when running the layout but the adjustable height means they could sit.

I daresay there are expert woodworkers who could make their wooden trestles do all this but most of us could not. In any case, their manufacture would add significantly to the construction time.

Figure 24 shows the assembled item, and you will also need the socket set we just used plus a cross-point screwdriver or the electric screwdriver turned down to low speed. The height is varied by first removing any load on top of the trestle, then removing the locking pins, which are secured by small chains. The vertical struts can then move up and down.

The struts are drilled with a number of holes and when you get the holes on both sides to line up, the pins can be put back with the strut in the new position. This is why it is important to remove any baseboard from the top before doing this.

The baseboards sit on top of the shiny crosspiece at the top of the structure and you can just see there are lugs sticking up that would stop boards sliding off the top surface. These lugs pivot out of the way for storage or transportation. The legs lock by what can only be described as the folding pushchair locking system, when a folding strut locks into position by being pulled down and gravity holds it locked, as well as a mechanical lock. In addition there is a further locking lever beneath the yellow warning triangle on both sides.

You should be able to see that the drilled holes in the uprights naturally face outwards, so they can receive the locking pins. When you get these items out of the box the vertical struts are fitted but turned inwards by 90 degrees and sometimes inverted, so make sure they are positioned as shown before you start to assemble the trestle. The vertical drilled struts have a 'pip' at the bottom of the strut that means you can only insert them from the bottom. This is to stop someone pulling the vertical strut upwards to make a height adjustment and the strut coming out of the housing completely.

Fig. 25 A trestle in the stowed position for transportation or storage.

The trestle is exactly 1m high from ground to top of crosspiece where the lugs are. This is about right for a person of medium height to stand at the layout but, of course, it is adjustable. The top cross-pieces, where the baseboards sit, are 685mm wide and well within our 610mm or 2ft baseboard width. The trestles are fitted with rubber feet inserts to protect vulnerable floors. Sometimes when work is being undertaken underneath the boards, fixed legs can get in the way and the trestles can be moved to one side for better access.

Figure 25 shows the stowed version, except for the aforementioned lugs, which fold down parallel with the top crosspiece. The unit is 33in (84cm) high.

If it is a serious intention to have a further board inserted, then two copies of the positions of the baseboard joiners can be taken now and stowed for safe-keeping or use the existing ends as fitted, as a template later on. It would be nice to say just drill it all to the same dimensions and it will fit, but this is optimism beyond reasonable bounds when working with basic hand tools.

Figure 26 is a picture of the boards assembled with the two 8mm bolts and all four trestles in position. The fiddle yard board is nearest; a piece of 9mm ply will be needed for the fiddle yard traverser deck.

Fig. 26 Both baseboards joined up and resting on the trestles.

Fig. 27   Wood block to steady the trestles.

Note how the trestles do not have any locators or locking yet; the former will be achieved by cutting 6in (150mm) pieces of rough-sawn timber and screwing them to the undersides of the existing framework. As well as providing locators for the trestles, they will also help lift the boards to stand off the floor when parked there. There are two issues here: first, when lifting the board onto the floor with an assistant, it is a case of 'mind your fingers' if the bottom of the boards are flush with the floor, and a similar problem exists when picking the boards off the floor. Second, there may be equipment, point and signal motors, and cabling, that may be damaged if there is not enough clearance between the underside of the board, where they are fitted, and the floor.

Figure 27 depicts the fiddle yard board upended and parked on top of the station board. The purpose

Fig. 28   Wood blocks doing their job.

of this manoeuvre is to position and screw down the 6in (150mm) blocks, which are going to be located in the trestles' crosspiece and stop any untoward movement. It was found that the crosspiece of the trestle was exactly the same width as an off-cut of the rough-sawn timber, i.e. 25mm or almost one inch. It is no good just using this as a guide and screwing down the blocks. The trestle crosspieces would be really difficult to fit, as the dimensions would be the same. The beer mat is a small additional spacer that allows the trestle crosspiece to slide in easily but does not allow the boards to slop or move about much.

The Dutch beer mat was chosen not so much for the intrinsic qualities of the beer, but for the thickness of the mat (although the beer is good). The 6in (150mm) blocks are pre-drilled with a 3mm drill and the 75mm decking screw or similar screwed in until the point of the screw is showing on the opposite side. Then, pointed side down, position the block as shown in Fig. 27 and lightly tap to locate the screws; this will stop the block from moving about whilst you are screwing it to the baseboard framing. If you are unsure, use the G-clamp we saw in Fig. 20 but

do not over-tighten or it will crush the wood. The station baseboards need two blocks but with the fiddle yard we used the bottom chipboard piece as one block.

Figure 28 shows both fiddle yard and station board block arrangements that hold the trestles securely and yet allow the boards to be lifted off easily. The fiddle yard trestle is the nearer.

As the decision is to go with the bought trestles, an £8 rebate was acquired from B&Q for one pack of rough-sawn timber returned.

TRACK AND POINT ISSUES

You can obtain a helpful view of whether the proposed points will fit on the layout at this stage, and even before you buy, online at the Peco website (http://www.peco-uk.com/page.asp?id=tempc75). This website provides track plans for all Peco code 75 points/turnouts or, in the USA, switches.

Figure 29 is the view from the fiddle yard towards the station buffer stops. The point plans were downloaded in PDF (Portable Document Format) from Peco's website, as above. They were then

Fig. 29 Point plans and track to see what will fit where.

Fig. 30   Initial track layout.

Fig. 31   Track and points sprayed in matt black.

printed out and trimmed to approximate to laying the actual points down. Also at this point (sorry!) you can move the plans into position so as to avoid the layout crosspieces that are running across the board and marked out by the countersunk screw heads in the picture. We already tried to factor this in and the points as laid out do not have a conflict. It just makes point motor installation simpler.

Figure 30 shows a dry run only with the actual points this time. The medium turnout was chosen as it was felt this gave the right blend of not looking like train-set track but managing to fit them in the space available. The track cannot be laid at this time as points need to have the wiring changed so that we can use relays to change the frog polarity, and it all needs painting first.

The sleepers are quite shiny and a fairly light shade of brown, which represents clean wood. In reality, the sleepers are not clean or shiny or light brown. It was decided to spray the sleepers matt black using Halfords' car paint at £7.99 for a 500ml tin – and a tin goes a fairly long way.

Figure 31 illustrates the garden shed with newspapers on the floor and the door open. The whole of the track so far is a double-slip, 5 points and 13 yards (11.9m) of track. It is not anticipated that the fiddle yard track will be painted. After this process the rails need to be painted a dirty rust colour and then all rail surfaces cleaned of paint. After the track has been laid down and got to work, the joints and disturbed areas can be touched in with paint.

Figure 32 illustrates a task that needs to be done before we can start track laying. All of the countersunk screws fitted in the chipboard surface need to be filled with decorator's filler and any excess smoothed off with medium-grade sandpaper. The tub on view cost about £1.50 and is ready mixed and, if the lid is kept secure when not in use, will last for months. The applicator is an old paint scraper but any type of flat-bladed implement, including a polypropylene one, would do. It takes a few hours to dry out thoroughly and the mix is generally a grey colour when wet and dries out to be white. You may consider newspapers or some sort of floor covering before this gets under way.

Fig. 32 Fill in where the screw heads are.

POINTS AND POINT ACTUATION CHOICE

Points are to be live frog in the sense that the whole unit is electrically live and so the frog has to be switched every time the point is changed over. The standard solution is to use the point blades and this works fine for a while but ultimately become unreliable. The point frog will, therefore, need to be switched by the point actuation.

Another consideration before track laying begins is the choice of point actuation. We will look at the options, and the pros and cons, and come up with a proposed solution based on the factors.

The term actuation was used in the heading rather than motor as there is a purely mechanical means that can be considered.

The wire-in-tube method consists of a small-diameter copper tube into which runs piano wire, which is a very tough and flexible stainless steel wire. The piano wire is connected to the point tie-bar and runs in the tube to the operating position. If the point lever is in fact a toggle switch, the switch can change the frog polarity.

Pros:

- Silent and reliable.
- Needs a fair bit of work to get it to work.
- Ideally suited to a single board shunting layout.

Cons:

- Baseboard joins a problem.
- Quite long distances a problem.
- Material costs high in recent years.

There are basically three types of point motor available on the market: the solenoid type, the motor-driven type or the servo.

A solenoid is a coil that has a mobile iron core within it that moves a short linear distance when a DC voltage is applied to the two terminals. The point motor version has two coils, one for each direction.

Pros:

- As there is usually only one moving part, they are very reliable.
- Consequently, they tend to be cheaper than other types.

Cons:

- Solenoids tend to operate rather quickly and points in real life tend to operate more slowly.
- Commercially available solenoids require a large hole to be made in the baseboard and if there is ever a problem with the motor, the point and surrounding track will need to be lifted. Not only will our track be secured but it will also be ballasted with fine granite chippings to represent the ballast on the prototype. Removal of a point motor that is buried is a considerable undertaking.
- They need to be pulsed to operate each coil separately and that introduces items like a capacitor discharge unit that has to supply a large jolt of electricity to move the motor core or passing contact switches that introduce unreliability.

- Frog switching can be problematic and may need a separate switch operated by the motor core.

The motor-driven types come from two manufacturers: Tortoise and Fulgurex. They both have a small DC motor that, through gearing, moves a shaft backwards and forwards. The shaft actuates small switches known as micro-switches to switch the motor off after it has reached the end of its travel in either direction and to prepare the circuit for the point motor's next selection. Tortoise point motors are about £17 currently and Fulgurex about £11.
Pros:

- Slower acting and more in keeping with prototype speed.
- Both types have auxiliary contacts that can be used for other purposes.
- Need just a toggle switch and two wire connections; no pulsing requirement.
- They do not need a large hole in the baseboard but the Tortoise still needs a slot cutting beneath the track.
- Simpler and more reliable frog switching.

Cons:

- Higher initial cost.
- Needs careful setting up.
- More complicated electrically and mechanically.

A servo device is a small motor and gearbox that moves only a small amount and it feeds back its current position to a controller circuit board. If the circuit board decides that the servo has moved enough, based on the feedback, it switches it off. The speed of movement, as well as range, is programmable by the user. One circuit board can control up to four servos.
Pros:

- Very controllable.
- Servos are reliable.
- Can be adapted to work other layout functions.

Cons:

- High unit cost of commercially available package, around £25 per point.
- Needs extra electronic board for live point frogs.
- Can be subject to electrical interference that causes them to judder unrealistically.

Although the servo solution is better, technically speaking, the cost and need to program circuit boards and such, whilst interesting to a computer studies' student, add a layer of complication at this stage.

Pulsed point motors are very reliable but the pulsing circuits and frog switching tends to let the motor down in the end.

Tortoise motors are very reliable and quiet but need a slot cutting in the baseboard for the operating arm and they cost more than Fulgurex. They are also somewhat bulky and require depth of space underneath the baseboard.

So, in the end, Fulgurex were chosen.

PREPARATION OF POINTS

At this juncture, it might be useful to look at some of the features of a prototype point and how they work on Network Rail.

Figure 33 is a pair of points outside Norton East Junction signal box near Stockton-on-Tees in Cleveland. The track farthest away, next to the signal box, which we can just see the bottom of, is a running line and trains go from left to right. The track nearest to the camera is another running line and trains go from right to left. The two parts of points in the picture are different in the sense that the nearer is a facing point. In earlier railway days, trains that face the sharp end of the point blades were sometimes known to force the blades apart and cause a derailment. Facing points were, therefore, avoided wherever possible, but where they were used, they were locked mechanically in whichever the selected position was. The grey box is a facing point lock mechanism and basically the tie-bar has two slots cut into it – one for each position of the blades. A rod at right angles to the rails

Fig. 33 Prototype point detail.

Facing Point Lock Mechanism

Point Tiebar

Point Blade

Stock Rail

locates in one of the slots to lock the point blades. The rods and bellcrank coming out from the box are the connection to the lever in the signal box to unlock the point blades so that they can be moved. After the point has been changed over, the facing point lock is replaced and it locates in the other slot in the tie-bar.

This is a mechanical setup, but electrically and hydraulically operated points have inbuilt facing point lock mechanisms and don't need a separate control. Single lines, as they are bi-directional, have many more facing points than on multiple running lines.

Facing point locks are not normally fitted on freight-only lines, but are where potentially hazardous loads are carried. Examples of this are bulk oil, chemicals and nuclear loads.

Note that the rails in Fig. 33 are anything from a rusty colour to black. The black here is caused by flange greasers that are fitted nearby, as there are very sharp curves at this junction.

The rods coming away from the tie-bar towards the camera go to a detection slide box, which makes sure that semaphore signals cannot be pulled off to 'clear' or 'off' if the point is in the wrong position. Points and signals can also be interlocked inside the signal box by a lever frame. We shall return to the subject of interlocking in the piece about signalling in Chapter 3.

The yellow bars connecting the point blades are 'stretcher bars' and they maintain the gauge of the rails but are not involved in the changing-over operation.

Before we can lay any points, they need to be prepared to ensure efficient and reliable operation with our chosen point motor:

- *Removal of the spring assembly.* Points are fitted with an 'over-centre' spring that is designed to snap into one position or the other. This spring needs to be removed for motor operation.
- *Operating lever arm for the point motor.* These point motors will have a small hole drilled into the baseboard and this will transmit the movement from under the baseboard where the point motor is to the point tie-bar. There needs to be a piece of brass wire to connect the tie-bar to the motor actuating lever.
- *Removal of mouldings used to mount the solenoid-type point motor.* These are extensions to the normal sleepers near the tie-bar that have slots cut into them to accommodate the Peco point motor. These will be removed, as they are unsightly and do not appear on the prototype.

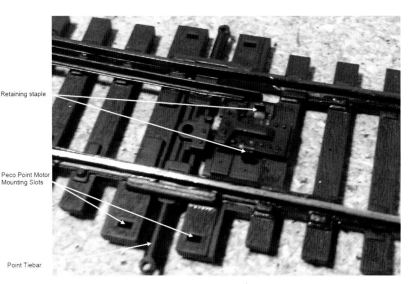

Retaining staple

Peco Point Motor
Mounting Slots

Point Tiebar

Fig. 34   Peco point detail.

• *Small change to the point wiring for live frog operation with a switch.* When you buy the live frog or 'Electrofrog' point it is wired so as to use the point blades to switch the power to the frog when the point changes. We need to change this arrangement so that an external switch is used for greater reliability.

Removal of the Spring Assembly

Figure 34 is an illustration of the operating area of the Peco Streamline point. What looks like a facing point mechanism, which we saw in Fig. 33, actually contains the over-centre spring that we need to remove.

The small moulding with the rivet heads is retained by a steel staple and the picture shows that

the legs of the staple have been turned upwards prior to removal. This was done with a Stanley knife blade, as a screwdriver does not have a thin enough blade to get under the staple to force the legs up. Make sure your fingers or any other part of your anatomy is not in the direction of where the blade might go!

Figure 35 is the view of the point inverted and the Stanley knife blade is used to gently lever the staple free. The facing point lock housing on the other side of the point will now fall away and within is the small spring. Carefully lever the spring out and make sure your eyes are not in the firing line, as the spring could leave its housing at a high Mach number and possibly exceed the speed of sound.

Collect the staple, spring and facing point lock cover, as they will go into the scrap box waiting for an opportunity for re-cycling. The facing point lock cover could easily be used again.

Operating Lever Arm

Figure 36 is the upturned point with the point actuating rod about to be fitted. This consists of a length of about 60mm of 0.8mm brass rod folded over with a pair of thin-nose or snipe nose pliers. The brass rod is available from K&S Metal Centers of Chicago, found in many model shops, or there are many dealers in metals on eBay.

Fig. 35   Peco point spring removal.

Fig. 36   Peco point actuating rod fitting.

The brass actuating rod will protrude underneath the tie-bar, so, to ensure free movement, we will have to hollow out the baseboard below the tie-bar to a depth of 3–4mm.

The operating eyes on the end of the tie-bar, as illustrated at Fig. 35, are an obvious facility but will give up after several hundred operations and all this is designed to last longer than that. Back to Fig. 36 again, and the eyes have been cut off as surplus to requirements. The actuating rod can be painted with rust colour after it has been trimmed to length in situ and fitted to the point motor.

Figure 37 is the actuating rod fitted and the point the right way up. The rod will pivot in the hole slightly to enable the connection to the point motor to be made or the brass rod can be bent to introduce a crank or displacement. Too much bending though, like any metal, and it will snap. Note how the point

blades have assumed the mid-position after the spring was removed in the previous operation.

Removal of Mouldings

This is done with the Stanley knife, as the slotted sleepers are quite thick and beefier than the usual crossing timbers – see Fig. 33 again. If the ends of the sleepers need trimming after the cutting process, use a small file or set of nail emery boards from a pound shop. They are perfectly alright for softer materials like sleepers.

Small Wiring Change

Figure 38 depicts the removal of two small links that will disconnect the point blades from the frog. With an Electrofrog point it is the blades that switch the frog but, as Peco point out, for greater reliability, do what we are doing now.

The implement in view is a Swann Morton scalpel, as used by the medical profession but also by modellers for many years. You can buy the blades separately and the blade on view is a no.21. The handle is a no.4. On Swann Morton's website it says you can use this combination for major surgical procedures but it does not mention that you can't use it for cutting Peco big sleepers – you need the Stanley knife for that. If a scalpel is used on something that is too thick or too tough, the blade will break. The scalpel is ideal for fine, light work. However, use great care with these items as they are very good at cutting skin and flesh.

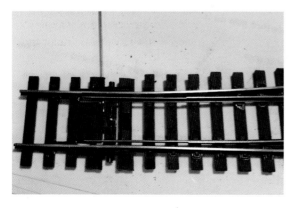

Fig. 37   Peco point actuating rod in position.

Fig. 38   Peco point switch rail link removal.

Fig. 39   Tinning copper wire.

The scalpel is used here to gently lever up the wire links before you can cut them off. The next part of the operation is to solder a link to each point blade connecting its adjacent rail. This will mean the blade will still be powered, even though we have cut the link. The first part of the process is to prepare a wire link to solder in position.

Figure 39 is a kind of recipe where we have solder and a soldering iron but also flux that will clean the area and make a better, stronger soldered joint. Any surface to be soldered needs to be as clean as you can get it for best results. The iron has to be of sufficient power to provide enough heat to get the solder to flow properly and the iron must have a steel tip covering the copper inner or it will corrode and fall off within weeks. The iron should be a minimum of 25W and preferably 40W. If you are ever in a situation where there is too much heat, any excess can usually be conducted away, so a higher wattage is always better. The tip must be clean and the usual way is to wipe it on a wet sponge. Those pan scourers that have a green abrasive pad on the sponge are good and they don't have to be new either.

In Fig. 39 there is a little solder on the iron tip and the reel is there to meet with the iron on the piece of wire to coat it in solder, after we have wiped it through the flux. This process of coating the copper wire with solder is referred to as 'tinning'.

You can see that part of the copper wire has already been tinned. The cable insulation needs to be stripped back first using a knife. Just cut lightly round the insulation, and not through the copper, and pull gently and the insulation will come off leaving the bare wire.

It takes a bit of practice to strip only the insulation. You can use commercially available wire strippers but by the time you've set up the jaws to only cut through to the diameter of cable conductor you have, you could have done the job with a knife. Wire strippers are good if you are doing a large number of cable ends of the same size.

More Health and Safety information in that the flux is mildly acidic as a cleaning agent, as are lots of household products, so do read all warnings and heed all precautions.

Solder is advertised as having resin flux cores in it already, but larger surfaces especially benefit from applying some more.

Resist the temptation to cut the wire up into links first, as the bit of wire with the insulation still on, as in Fig. 39, will give you something to handle the wire with and it will get hot.

Fig. 40   Peco point links in position.

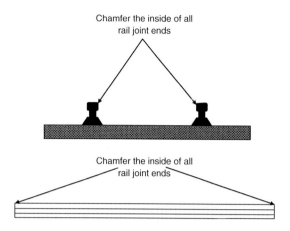

Fig. 41   Rail treatment before laying the track.

Turn the point upside down and scrape the exposed rail underneath with a knife. Place a dab of flux on each scraped piece of rail and gently dab the iron and solder — this is tinning the rail.

As in Fig. 40, place the wire across the rail and dab with the iron and a good joint should flow straight away. If it does not, usually, the iron is not hot enough. After both rails have been soldered, any excess wire can be trimmed with a pair of miniature side-cutters.

The links will be visible when the point has been laid so we must remember to go round with the paint brush, to touch in when we know it is all working. It is possible some of the ballast will obscure the links.

TRACK LAYING

Before we lay the track, we need a decision about a track base. A track base will raise the track above ground level and make it appear higher than the surrounding ground. This is fine for high-speed main lines and indeed essential. However, lower speed — mainly freight — lines tend not to be so banked up; Fig. 33 for an example. This means our track on our branch line will not have a track base and this, by the way, will accentuate the width of the track.

Now that the track has been prepared for laying, we can put it down. Initially the track will be positioned and any cuts in the flexible track made to accommodate position or curvature and the whole thing lightly pinned down. Then cuts in the rail for electrical purposes will have to be done and point

motors positioned. After trains have run over all the tracks, the track can be ballasted and secured. The pins used to lightly secure the track in position can subsequently be removed or painted over if they are unsightly.

When derailments on plain track are investigated it is usually found to be a rail joint out of alignment and very often on a curve, as the rail joint ends are trying to straighten up and not go round a curve. The fishplates do a good job on straight track but they do not curve themselves. Either the wheel tread hits a rail head sticking up or a flange hits the inside of a rail end that is not fully aligned.

Figure 41 shows what we can do about this in terms of rail preparation. After we have cut the rail to length to fit in the location, slightly round the tops of rail ends and the inside of rail ends — the technical name for this is chamfering. This is done with either a small file or emery boards. All we are looking to do is to remove the sharp edge.

INITIAL POSITIONING OF TRACK AND POINTS

We are going to start off with the double-slip as that is the pivotal point on the whole layout. It will be easier for all other trackwork to fan out from the double-slip, rather than lay the rest of it first and then try to connect with the double-slip afterwards. There will be those who will want it drawn

Fig. 42   Making rebates for the actuating rods.

out on the boards first, and that is fine but time-consuming.

First we position the double-slip on the board and we have to be mindful that one of the tracks needs to be close to the centre line of the baseboards, as the tracks must all line up with the traverser. (A traverser is a sliding deck that moves at right angles to a track and allows access to multiple tracks – see Fig. 72.)

Mark off the ends of the sleepers where the tie-bars are with a felt-tip pen.

Figure 42 introduces another gadget, described as a rotary multi-tool. This is quite often referred to as a Dremel, as that is the tradename in the USA where these things originate – rather like the name Hoover. It can be a drill, a rotary file, a cutter and so on. In the case shown it is a rotary file and it has been used to make a rounded slot into which

the tie-bars of the double-slip will fit and move easily. This operation generates a fair amount of dust but is soon finished with; it takes seconds.

The double-slip comes with pieces of wire called 'droppers', as their purpose is to connect to track feeds below the baseboards. There are four connections altogether and you mark where they will drop with a felt-tipped pen and then drill 3mm. The drill size is more than plenty big enough but it is wise to allow for the hole you have just drilled not being perfectly aligned with the wire.

Figure 43 is the double-slip lightly pinned down after we have checked that the tie-bars are free to move easily. The slight bend in the brass actuating rods has been introduced, as we will wish to run stock over the laid track to make sure all is well. The bend in the rod impinges on the baseboard and stops the point blades from moving as we are running stock through. Note that the brass pins used to secure the double-slips have protruding heads; they have not been tapped all the way in. If we need to remove these later, there is enough to grab hold of with the pliers; if we batter them in at this stage, they will be very difficult to remove. The only practical way, other than gently lifting the track up, is to grind the head of the pin off with the rotary tool, but beware sleeper damage.

Figure 44 is an overview of the basic tools used in the track laying. The hammer is known as a jeweller's ball pein and all hammers are sold by the weight of the head of the hammer you are doing

Fig. 43   Double-slip pinned in position.

Fig. 44   Track pins and the tools.

the bashing or, in this case, tapping with. Deep-rooted in the Victorian age, which produced railways in the first place, they are known as 1 ounce or 2 ounce, which would translate to a metric equivalent of 28g or 56g, although they are not sold as a metric value in the UK.

The snipe-nosed pliers are used to hold the track pins whilst you wield the hammer. This means that you will avoid collateral damage to your fingers but

also, as you are holding the track pin rigid, it is less likely to buckle in half, even though you are only lightly tapping it.

The track pins themselves are brass and are sold as escutcheon or miniature pins on eBay, but you can use ordinary track pins.

Figure 45 is an illustration of a solution rather than a problem. When we come to lay track that is meeting at a point, the track is not configured

Sleepers that have been cut and removed

Mark 2 version of the temporary point lever

Fish plates Need touching in after track is secured with ballast

*Fig. 45
Temporary point
changeover.*

Fig. 46 Cutting sleeper webs to interleave track.

to fit exactly with the track next to it. The sleeper spacing has been pre-determined in the moulding process and is correct for plain track.

The point at the bottom of the figure has two tracks coming into it, one of which is another point on the left. We cannot modify the point easily so the sleepers of the plain track must be made to interweave with what is already there on the adjacent point. The sleepers highlighted in Fig. 45 are those removed and modified so that they will fit with adjacent tracks and look right.

Figure 46 depicts a piece of track inverted and the web, or plastic moulding, that holds the sleepers together but at a distance, has been cut roughly with the Stanley knife.

In the example shown in Fig. 45, there are four sleepers removed and refitted after the track has been laid and it depends on how shallow the angle is that the tracks meet. If the angle is very shallow, then more sleepers will overlap and more have to be cut. If you don't get it right, all it means is that you have to remove the track and take more sleepers off.

Some sleepers will need to be removed completely as you will not be able to join the tracks up with some sleepers still in place near the fish plates.

The small file depicted was used to chamfer the rail ends.

Figure 47 is an ultra 'warts and all' close-up of a cut sleeper and in the example in Fig. 45, we needed

four of these. The chairs have been cut off with the Swann Morton knife as they would tend to force the track upwards if we just shoved them in as they are. The chair bases remain, as that is what the rail normally sits on. Don't worry if you cut the chair bases off though, as this would not be apparent when assembled.

These are then slotted in after the rails are joined up with fishplates. These free-moving sleepers can either be secured with a touch of impact adhesive, like UHU, or pinned down with track pins. This is necessary otherwise the carefully placed and spaced loose sleepers will be displaced by the ballasting process.

Fig. 47 A trimmed sleeper to interleave.

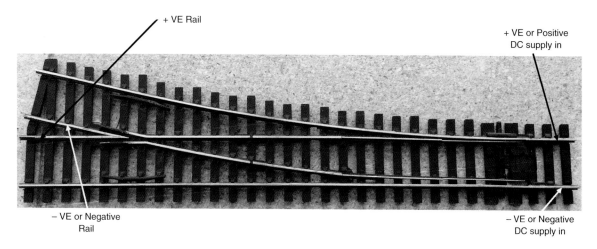

+ VE Rail

+ VE or Positive
DC supply in

− VE or Negative
Rail

− VE or Negative
DC supply in

Fig. 48   A Peco point and how the polarity changes when the blades change.

Figure 48 is an illustration of the issues surrounding wiring and connecting the track we have just laid. In Fig. 48, if we make an assumption that the top rail will be DC positive and the bottom rail DC negative we can work out what has to happen to the point frog electrically for it to work when the point is selected to a different position. It will change round if the locomotive is reversed but for now we will consider this situation. In addition, if the layout is using DCC it will be fed with AC but as the same problem exists in either case, it is simpler to illustrate with DC analogue.

If the points are set as shown for the straight track, then the frog has to be positive polarity to maintain a straight run through of the train.

If the points are then changed to operate on the curved track towards the top-left of the picture, then the frog needs to be negative to ensure a straight run through. Clearly then the frog polarity must be switched every time the points are changed.

There is a subsidiary issue and that is, that whichever selection is made, there will be a short-circuit on the non-switched side, and we must introduce rail breaks to avoid that. Peco recommend that you buy their insulated rail joiners but that is extra cost and extra work. In addition, they look a bit odd.

Figure 49 is the answer to rail breaks in the form of the rotary multi-tool fitted with a cutting disc.

Fig. 49   Cutting track for electrical integrity.

USE SAFETY GLASSES

The discs are brittle and shatter easily so always wear safety glasses; they are about £1.50 from B&Q and are far cheaper than new eyes, which the NHS isn't currently funding.

The breaks can be positioned away from the frog such that a point can form a section break where a locomotive can be held. This is a useful feature but there is a matter that needs observation. If a metal wheeled item of rolling stock is bridging the gap between sections that are meant to be separate or insulated, there will be a short-circuit caused and it would only require the wheel to be moved off the joint for the short-circuit to disappear.

The cutting discs are various sizes and so the slot size can vary, but cutting them this size will introduce the clickety-click feature of a train running over the gaps, if you have metal-wheeled stock. Continuous welded rail (CWR) does not have this feature but the two single-track branch lines would not necessarily be equipped with CWR and probably not.

The precise position of the cuts and associated track feeds will be covered in Chapter 3, together with a revised track plan.

FIDDLE YARD TRAVERSER

The precise height of the traverser can only be arrived at after the approach tracks from the station board have been laid. Structures made of wood are often like that.

The traverser deck is a piece of 9mm ply cut to size by those nice people at B&Q at no extra charge. It is 1,210mm by 607mm – this is the width needed to accommodate six tracks of storage, although in effect it will be five when you make allowance for a run-round road for the freight trains. The piece of plywood was cut in half and then had 10mm cut off the ends, so there are actually two pieces of fiddle yard deck, only one of which is used. This was the most economical way but the original piece of plywood was £20. The other half of the plywood was subsequently used to cover all rolling stock in the fiddle yard. (As the layout was built in a conservatory, the stock needed protection from direct sunlight.)

It is 9mm plywood when the baseboard deck is 12mm for a very good reason. The traverser will need something to slide on and maintain it at right angles to the incoming tracks. A traverser deck 12mm thick would slide on wood and this sticky arrangement could cause jerky movements of the traverser and pitch the rolling stock off the tracks. Conversely, a traverser deck that runs on rails

Fig. 50 Fiddle yard traverser deck.

Fig. 51 Fiddle yard traverser deck on sliders.

and roller bearings may be prone to running across the tracks too quickly and banging into the end stop with the same rolling stock outcome. Not only that, but it is more work to get it to operate properly.

The other issue to bear in mind is that our traverser will accommodate two incoming tracks and each of those must align with any of the six roads. This means the traverser will need to go beyond the far edge of the baseboard frame.

Figure 50 depicts the basic piece of 9mm ply to which has been added two pieces of rough-sawn timber from the original purchase as framing. In this case the framing is at rail level but the framing provides a handle to move the traverser across on the one hand and a safety rail to stop rolling stock pitching off the far end at the other.

The six tracks are laid roughly in position at this point. There is no crosswise framing underneath the plywood traverser deck at this point until we know what the arrangement for the traverser sliding mechanism is to be.

Figure 51 shows the traverser deck mounted in position but it is riding on five aluminium angle extrusions, which are cut to a length of slightly less

than 22in (555mm). This ensures that they do not have to be forced into position, which would cause the traverser deck to rise up and therefore not align with the incoming tracks. It also takes account of any issue with temperature expansion. The off-cut in the well of the traverser deck will be used for a guide to keep the traverser deck at right angles to the incoming tracks.

The 19 × 19mm aluminium extrusion is sold in 800mm lengths and can be bought from eBay for £2 each piece for this size. We need five pieces: three to sit on the baseboard framing and the two ends. The total is £12, including postage.

It is 1.6mm thick so this means we have to theoretically find another 1.4mm before the traverser deck is level with the baseboards. As we are working on wood, it may be more or less in actual fact. The next size up in extrusions is thicker than 3mm.

Thick card happens to be 1.4mm and was cut into strips and introduced between the fiddle yard wood frame and the aluminium extrusions. This should now make the two surfaces of the baseboards and fiddle yard traverser deck the same. However, we can fine tune this later.

Fig. 52   Cutting aluminium guides.

Fig. 53   Aluminium guide tools.

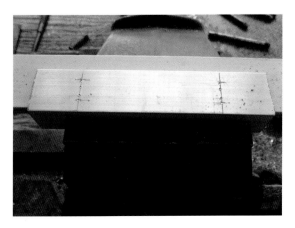

Fig. 54   Slot-making, step 1.

CAUTION

Aluminium produces lots of waste material from the drilling process known as swarf and it can be sharp, so be careful when handling the work.

Aluminium is one of those metals that will not solder using conventional soldering equipment, but that property will not trouble us here. Figure 52 illustrates the start of the production of four aluminium guides, which are going to help the traverser board slide across and line up with the incoming tracks. The offcuts from the extrusions were about 4in (100mm) long, which is fine for what we want. If yours are not that, cut them to size with a hacksaw. A junior hacksaw is about £2 with blades and the more grown-up frame hacksaw is under £10, both from eBay. As we are cutting aluminium, which is a relatively soft metal, a junior hacksaw will do.

The guides will need slots cutting in them so that we can adjust the way the traverser slides across the board. You will need a vice to hold everything with and these vary from £10 upwards; a second-hand one on eBay is usually a good buy as these items don't really wear out – 3in (75mm) jaws will be the right size.

Figure 52 depicts a 4in (100mm) piece of the extrusion used as a template or pattern to cut further items from. Aluminium is so soft that the serrated jaws of the vice will leave their mark on the metal, so if this concerns you, put some stout cardboard in the jaws before you clamp them up on the piece we are cutting. These guides will be underneath the traverser deck, so maybe it doesn't matter that much.

Figure 53 shows a few more tools to help us produce the slots for the aluminium guides for the traverser deck. The hammer needs to be used gently with aluminium. The engineer's square or L-shaped gadget will help draw perpendicular lines using the machined edges of the aluminium. The pointy thing is a scribe and that will put a permanent line on the material, which we will use to define where we are to drill. The fourth tool is a centre punch that will accurately mark and provide a guide for the drill. The steel rule will not only measure, but join up marks with the scribe.

The 4in (100mm) aluminium guide ready to be drilled is shown in Fig. 54. Marking out is as follows:

1. Measure ¾in (20mm) from each end and mark with the scribe.
2. Translate the mark into a perpendicular line by using the engineer's square held against the machined angle of the aluminium.
3. Mark off two further sets of lines ⅕in (5mm) from the edges.
4. Using the hammer and centre punch, make four 'pops' or indentations into the metal on the perpendicular lines and within the last two lines marked out.
5. Finally, drill 3mm holes on all popped marks.

Fig. 55   Slot-making, step 2.

Fig. 56   Slot-making, step 3.

Figure 55 is the drilled guide, and the use of the piece of scrap wood underneath the guide becomes clear. Most vices are extremely hard and would break a drill if they came into contact with it, so the wood protects the drill. If your vice is made of aluminium, as some woodworkers' vices are, the wood will protect the vice.

The guide can then be removed from the vice and then remounted such that the guide is held by the end only. This will enable you to replace the drill and work it up and down in the direction of the originally drawn perpendicular line, so as to break the gap between the drilled holes and so produce a slot.

Figure 56 depicts the left-hand slot that has had the extra treatment from the drill, as just described, and the right-hand slot is being finished off with files to accept the screw shown, which is a no.8 ½in (12mm). These were in stock and should strictly speaking be round headed, but these too will be out of sight so it doesn't matter that much. They can't be any longer than 12mm as the traverser deck is only 9mm but we are not countersinking them so the screws will not protrude onto the trackside of the deck. The screws will come in handy for securing point and signal motors; a box is about £2 from either Toolstation or Screwfix.

Fig. 57   Slot-finishing tools.

Fig. 58   Slotted guide in use as a template.

You widen the slots out until the screw just fits and the countersunk head stands proud.

Figure 57 is a picture of the tools needed to achieve the slot widening. They are described as jeweller's needle files and are also available on eBay for about £2 a set of six. They become clogged up with softer materials, as shown, but you can use a fine-wire brush to remove the bits.

We have now gone to quite a bit of trouble to produce an adjustable guide but we will need four. Figure 58 shows the start of the production process, where the prototype is used once again as a pattern or template. This time, just drill through the slots of the master, which is then removed, so that the slots can be enlarged and shaped, as before.

Figure 59 demonstrates the drilling process under way; the first two holes to be drilled are the top and bottom of the slot. If you are using an electric drill, start off the hole very slowly until you are sure the hole is going to be where you want it – this takes the place of the centre punch operation we did for the prototype or master. If the swarf becomes a nuisance, brush it away with an old domestic paintbrush.

With all four of the guides fabricated, we can now offer them up to the traverser deck for a fitting, bearing in mind that the screws needed to attach

Fig. 59   Slotted guide in use as a template after drilling.

Fig. 60   Traverser deck line up.

the guides will be positioned some way along the slot to enable adjustments to be made.

Before we can offer up the guides and screw them down, the traverser deck has first to be centralized because there will be storage roads at both ends and so vehicles need to run off at both ends (Fig. 60). The gap in total is only about 2–3mm and here it is taken up by two pieces of card at each end, such that the traverser deck will just still move but there is no measurable tendency of the deck to slop about. In other words, it moves, as near as we can make it, parallel to the chipboard ends.

Then offer up one of the guides, so that it is lightly bearing on the aluminium runner at one of the ends, and mark off with a felt-tipped pen (Fig. 61). Then do the same with the guide at the other side of the same end. Referring back to Fig. 60, this is the same end nearest the camera, on the left, but towards the window.

When we come to fit the guide on this location, nearest the window, it will be inboard of the traverser deck edge because the deck will need to slide over to line the nearest track on the deck with the farthest incoming road. If we mounted the guide at the far edge, it would hit the far side of the baseboard frame before the deck would line up.

Repeat the process with the opposite end, which, referring back to Fig. 60 again, is the end furthest away from the camera.

The two sets of felt-tipped pen marks can be joined up to form lines that are about ¾in (20mm) from the ends of the deck at both ends.

Figure 62 shows the traverser deck upended so the nearest edge normally is now near the window or furthest from the camera. The guides have been

Fig. 61   Traverser deck guide fitted.

Fig. 62   Traverser deck guide adjustment.

Fig. 63   Traverser deck guide lubrication.

screwed down with the no.8 ½in (12mm) wood-screws, and the process to keep the guides in contact with the aluminium runners is under way. The woodscrews securing the guides are lightly screwed in at this point.

The woodscrews on their own by the guides are sophisticated adjustment and locking devices. The screws are cone-shaped and by screwing them in, the guide is forced a small amount towards its runner. When the optimum setting is found by the easy sliding of the deck across the runners, tighten up the guide-securing screws. The screw on its own now becomes a locking device, as the only place the guide can go is towards the camera or away from the runner. The locking screws are only fitted when you are close to achieving an easy sliding motion and act as a form of final adjustment.

Note that the guide nearest the camera, which is the one furthest away when the deck is right way up, is inboard of the deck edge; as we indicated when discussing Fig. 61, about 3in (75mm) is enough.

Fig. 64   Traverser deck under-framing.

Figure 63 introduces the concept of 'witness marks'. This is a term borrowed from the world of forensic science, where evidence of what has happened at a crime scene is derived from marks left by people or things. The most obvious example perhaps is skid marks at a road traffic collision. The issue we have is that it is difficult to determine what if any part of the guide is in contact with the runners and if so where.

In a model railway context we can use grease, smeared along the surface of the guides to determine how effectively they are in contact with the runners. The marks left by the grease act as witness marks to tell us what adjustments to make. Petroleum jelly is just as effective and is available from pharmacies or supermarkets. The grease also acts as a lubricant.

Now that the guides are in place and have been adjusted to our satisfaction, the underside of the traverser deck can be strengthened with cross-framing. Figure 64 shows one of the four framing pieces needed, and once again it is part of the rough-sawn timber originally bought cut to a length of 9½in (240mm). Note that we are using the framing with the narrow edge to the deck, as the wood is the most rigid in this position. There is no chance of the wood fouling the bottom of the traverser chipboard, as the deck is lifted off the runners by the aluminium strip and card packing pieces to about 3mm.

The framing is secured close to the end of the deck, as the guides will allow and still have access to adjust the guides. This is required because the most critical part of operating the movement of rolling stock will be over the track joints near the deck ends.

The framing is first secured with a 75mm decking screw or chipboard screw. These types of screw are chosen because they are thin and, if a 3mm pilot hole is drilled, will not split the timber it is affixed to. It is 75mm long because the screw has to go through the 38mm framing, then the 9mm chipboard deck, then into the longitudinal 38mm framing on the other side of the deck. This is the only one that does this on the one frame. Chipboard or decking

Fig. 65   Traverser deck under-framing in use.

screws can be bought in small quantities from eBay for under £2.

The framing timbers are cut to 9½in (240mm) so as not to stop the traverser deck from reaching over to access the far tracks on the deck for both incoming tracks. As we can see, the framing stops about the same distance short as the guides.

Measure from the deck edge to the edge of the framing timber and in this case the value is 2¾in (70mm). Repeat this down the length of the framing piece to ensure it is at right angles to the deck edge. Turn the board over and, allowing to add 12mm to drill right into the centre of the framing (see Fig. 65), drill a 3mm pilot hole. Then secure with a 40mm screw from the tub of 1,000 we originally bought.

Repeat this for the other three framing, securing screws, all at 3¼in (82mm) from the deck edge, in this case.

The traverser deck is the right way up once more (Fig. 65) and is at the fullest extent of its travel 'towards the window' (or away from the operator), to show how far it has to go to allow both incoming tracks to access all traverser tracks.

The crosswise framing is repeated at intervals between the runners and at the far end. This means another three framing pieces like the one shown.

Note how the nearer incoming track on the left has been secured at its end with a piece of 'copper-clad' sleeper. This is highly adjustable and much more robust than the plastic sleepered track. The further track has not been secured yet with the copper-clad sleeper but will be when the traverser tracks are laid. Both tracks have been fine-tuned by filing the ends of the rails such that they are the same length and do not protrude towards the traverser deck too much.

Copper-clad sleepers can be found at Marcway of Sheffield, who now market the former SMP (Scale Model Products) range of such equipment. One-hundred sleepers were £6.50 at the time of writing.

The traverser deck must not only be locked in position, but power must be connected to the selected track and definitely by the same action.

Figure 66 shows the potential solution to both problems. On the left is a sliding cupboard door bolt, which is in moulded and machined brass but is chromium plated. It is, however, a precise sliding mechanism and, with modification, it will provide a rigid lock to the traverser and line a track up and connect it electrically. The bolt head has been filed down, as the bolt will be fitted near to the track and the bolt head would foul a passing vehicle unless so modified.

Fig. 66   Traverser deck lock, cupboard door bolts.

Fig. 67   Traverser deck lock, cupboard door bolts'
modification.

The bolt, as supplied, has a 'captive' function that means the bolt cannot slide out of its housing under normal use. We will not be using the bolt normally and the bolt will need to be released from captivity. Place the bolt housing vertically on a rigid surface, such as a vice jaw, such that the sliding bolt with the knob on points downward. Hold the bolt in this position and strike the sliding bolt with a centre punch and hammer. Resistance will be felt but after a firm tap the sliding bolt will slide all the way down and out of the housing. The brass insert that holds the sliding bolt captive will fall out and this needs to go in the scrap box until we can find a use for it.

The right-hand view of Fig. 66 shows the bolt slider separated from its housing and you can see the channel in which the brass insert sat to restrict movement. The housing will be needed to hold not only the bolt, but two 15mm pieces will be marked and sawn off to use as traverser deck locating locks.

Figure 67 is a 'before' and 'after' shot in the sense that the lower bolt is before splitting and the upper one after splitting and sawing. The housing does not lend itself to marking out with a ruler and scribe. Locate one end of the housing lightly clamped in the vice and slide the bolt in to where the jaws are holding the housing. This is to avoid the possible deformation of the housing by the vice jaws. Hold the steel ruler ⅜in (15mm) from the free end and draw a hacksaw blade backwards to make a mark. Take the ruler away and carefully locate the

hacksaw blade in the mark we have just made and rock it to make another mark on the other side of the housing. Once you have a satisfactory pair of marks, saw off the ⅜in 15mm piece, which will go on the traverser deck. Repeat once more and we then have a cut-down housing for the sliding bolt and two traverser deck locks. Note the centre punch in Fig. 67. There will only be a screw hole in the first piece you cut off, so you will need to centre pop and drill 3.5mm as near to the centre of the channel as possible (see Fig. 66 centre of the picture). There is not enough room to get a countersink bit in there, but if the screw is sitting in the channel, all will be well and the sliding bolt will not catch on the screw head.

Figure 68 demonstrates sawing a ⅜in 15mm piece from the bolt housing. Place a steel rule against the side of the vice jaw and also place the housing until the end lines up with the ⅜in 15mm mark on the rule. Clamp the housing lightly in the vice and, using the side of the vice as a guide, saw through the housing, as shown in Fig. 68. The hacksaw will not saw through the vice or even mark it.

Clearly we need a total of three bolts to furnish us with enough traverser deck locks for the six tracks on the traverser. The left-over sliding bolt and any other pieces will be squirreled away as spares.

When there are six traverser locks and two sliding bolts, we can start to install a locking mechanism on the tracks. First, lay six pieces of track and evenly space them out so that you can see how six tracks will fit and still leave room for stock to get past each other and avoid the sidewalls of the wooden

Fig. 68   Cupboard door bolts, cutting up slider.

*Fig. 69   Traverser
deck lock first fitting.*

framing. Mark both ends of where the tracks will go with a felt-tipped pen. This operation will give you the space needed to fit the traverser locks between the tracks, and the sleepers where those locks are must be trimmed. In addition, it is better if the sleepers at the end are copper-clad. Copper-clad sleepers will put up with many more accidental knocks and bumps, and rails can be re-aligned with the touch of a soldering iron. Copper-clad sleepers enable us to fine-tune the track joint where traverser meets baseboard.

Copper-clad sleepers can be cut with a sharp pair of side-cutters but will need a circuit break, between the rails, cutting with a file. They may need packing underneath with thick card, as the sleepers will be thinner than Peco-moulded plastic ones, but this is a judgement call when you get the rails lined up.

Figure 69 shows the second track traverser lock about to be installed, but the first one is also in view and we can see the process.

RUNNING-IN TRACK AND SLIDING BOLT

1. Trim sleepers back to the chairs and make the last one copper-clad, securing it with a 12mm panel pin through a 1.5mm drilled hole. Sometimes you will need two holes and two panel pins to get the track to sit right. You can always fine-tune by moving the rail and re-soldering in the new position.

2. Position the bolt housing such that the end is up to the baseboard end but no further. Secure the bolt housing with two of the screws supplied with the bolt – the larger one is illustrated in Fig. 69. When you are screwing in the second screw nearest the track, wind round the screw a 75mm piece of 0.5mm thick brass wire. This is sold as Gauge 25 SWG, which stands for Standard Wire Gauge or as Gauge 24 AWG, which is American Wire Gauge but is actually 0.5mm in diameter. It costs about £2.50 for 15m from eBay and is advertised as suitable for snaring rabbits.

3. Trim the brass wire so that you can solder the end to the copper-clad sleeper.

4. Take the sliding bolt and file down any edges. Fit the sliding bolt and ensure it slides freely.

5. Line the traverser locking housing up with the sliding bolt, as shown in Fig. 69, but we are still on the first track. Ensure that the track on the traverser deck will line up with the running-in track; if it doesn't, then trim some more off the sleepers until it does. It will not be secured yet until we have the deck locked.

6. Screw in a no.8 ½in (12mm) screw into the baseboard behind the sliding bolt, as shown in Fig. 69 on the left. This acts as an end-stop

for the sliding bolt so it will not fall out of the housing if withdrawn too quickly. Caution: because the sliding bolt mechanism is the one to which all traverser tracks must match and line up with, once it is in position, it must not be altered or adjusted in any way.

7. Take another of the larger screws supplied with the cupboard door lock and cut it back to be about ⅖in (10mm) long. The traverser deck is only 9mm thick, so the screws, as supplied, are too long but, allowing for the thickness of the housing, 10mm should fit. Drill the traverser deck to a depth of about ⅕in (5mm) and screw in the now modified screw, first ensuring that there is another piece of brass wire underneath the housing. Ensure that the bolt slides all the way in. Then take a no.8 ½in (12mm) screw and screw it in partially, as shown in Fig. 69. This acts as an end-stop for the sliding bolt, a device to lock the housing piece in position and a form of adjustment for the position of the housing. Be careful not to screw it all the way in. If you find the brass wire upsets the housing height, wrap the brass wire round the no.8 screw; there will be an electrical contact through the housing.

8. When you have a locking traverser deck, now is the time to offer up the track to line up with the running-in line. Before any traverser track is fitted, the ends of the track must be the same lengths. After that a copper-clad sleeper can be soldered in so that the ends will not then move relative to one another.

9. Drill and panel pin the traverser track in position and check for clearances with your largest and widest stock item. Provided they are to the British loading gauge, it should fit.

10. Secure the remaining part of the track with pins and add another 12in (300mm) or so to extend the tracks to the end of the traverser deck, checking that the track remains the same distance from the wooden framing all the way along. Solder the brass wire from the housing to the copper clad, as before. The brass wire from the first track can just be seen in Fig. 69.

11. Connect a cable from the far rail, which will act as a common wire joining all six tracks by that one far rail. The nearer rails are switched by the traverser deck mechanism.

And it lives! The single car Northern Rail DMU class 153 is powered through the traverser deck lock (Fig. 70). The snow plough is the nearest part of the DMU to the cupboard door bolt mechanism.

It was subsequently discovered that the black steps hanging down on the class 153 just fouled the sliding bolt handle but did not derail. The no.8 screw nearest the camera in Fig. 70 was removed, the bolt

Fig. 70 Class 153 tries out the first traverser track.

Fig. 71   Two-track deck lock before adjustments.

Fig. 72   Traverser deck lock, only one at once.

slid out and some more brass chamfered off the bolt handle.

Connect the power supply controller temporarily to the running-in rails and make sure the common wire referred to in Step 11 is connected to the far rail; check stock runs over the traverser deck satisfactorily. Note that the traverser deck tracks, as they are not part of the scenic railway, have not been sprayed black nor the rails painted.

Steps 7 to 11 need to be repeated for all other traverser tracks before we can install the other running line sliding bolt.

A start is made to install the sliding bolt on the far running track (Fig. 71). This time, instead of using the slider as the starting point, it is now the end point. In other words, we begin with the deck lock, which we have just fixed into position, and mate the sliding bolt up to that. The question as to which one out of the six is a vexed one, but the one that was a best fit was selected.

In Fig. 71, the running-in track has a copper-clad base now but the rails are not soldered down and won't be until the sliding bolt is fitted. Similarly, the rail ends need trimming. As the sliding bolt and its housing are just sitting there at present, we need to ensure that the housing will not move when we remove the bolt to drill for the securing screws. A pair of panel pins either side will hold the bolt housing in position.

Also to be noted is that the original track no longer lines up, while we have the far track, shown,

lined up. This is intentional and essential, as much chaos would otherwise be caused.

Figure 72 shows that the bolt housing is affixed, rails soldered down to fit and trimmed, and the Freightliner class 66 is making its way onto the running line. To the right of the housing can just be seen a blob of solder, which is securing the piece of brass wire we are using to connect to the adjacent rail; it is where one of the panel pins is situated. The new sliding bolt under test does not have its countersunk screw end-stop yet, as its forerunner has.

Note that the far right-hand track has a little more room width-wise between the tracks but basically it all just fits.

If angled steel bracing had been used instead of the rough-sawn timber, we may have squeezed in a seventh track, but that adds a further layer of complexity and cost, as well as weight.

The track that the class 66 is on, and the next two to its right, had their right-hand running rails cut to divide the roads up into two. This means we can accommodate two 2-car DMUs on each track or a light engine as well as a DMU. The DMUs will be at the far side of the fiddle yard from the operator, as we will not need to do any coupling or uncoupling of these units.

The running sequence must reflect the storage of stock in the sense that we don't want our next move on the sequence to be boxed in behind another DMU, say, in front of the train we want. Operators will need to be aware of such issues to keep it all

Fig. 73   Sliding cupboard-door bolt modification.

running smoothly and this adds to the satisfaction to be gained. Such issues form part of running the real railway.

In terms of freight trains, it is envisaged, at this stage, that there will be two full and one empty limestone trains.

The reason that this model of cupboard door bolt was chosen (*see* Fig. 73) is that it is a precise sliding fit and, in terms of our application, a little too precise. The plywood deck is wood and that moves and changes on its own. The image on the left of Fig. 73 shows a bolt profile where the shape has been eased, compared with the new one on the right and this will give us an easier lead in when making a track connection. The rest of the sliding part of the bolt is unchanged. Note also the cut-down housing, as we have taken some of it for the traverser deck locks.

Figure 74 is a picture of work in progress at the other end of the fiddle yard with the track joints visible. The fishplates have been soldered to both rails and the far rail has the black cable to connect all far rails to it. The other rail is always powered by the sliding cupboard door bolt, which of course means that the tracks must always line up before any rolling stock rolls.

There are other tracks to be laid in the fiddle yard to accommodate run-round facilities.

RUN-ROUND TRACKS AND A DIFFERENT SLIDING BOLT

There are four tracks laid beyond the traverser deck, which are about 12in (300mm) long – sufficient for a class 66. Each road needs a connection and locking mechanism to the traverser deck.

Figure 75 shows the kit of parts that will be needed to construct the traverser deck locking and power catches for the run-off tracks at the end of the traverser roads. When a freight train arrives on either of the two incoming tracks, the locomotive will need to be either temporarily stored or run round the train so as to take up its next duty.

The bases of the locking and power catches are a copper-clad material, only this time it is in sheet form and is sold on eBay as 'pcb', where pcb stands for 'printed circuit board'.

Electronic circuits as found in smartphones and tablets are laid out and connected using a board that has the circuit etched into the surface and often the

Fig. 74   Fiddle yard traverser isolating sections.

Fig. 75   Fiddle yard loco track-locking catches – materials.

board is multi-layered to accommodate complex inter-layer connections. The basis of this function, in its crudest form, is sold for people to make their own simpler circuits. However, it is useful in a model railway context and not particularly expensive at £2.99 for a sheet measuring 100mm by 200mm.

1. Mark out the sheet into a matrix of 15mm by 10mm rectangles, measuring four by three, making twelve rectangles in all. We shall need eight for our four tracks but it is as easy to do more and we may need spares in the future. We need to use the steel rule and set square, as used before.

2. Drill the rectangles along their short sides with a 1.25mm drill; this is to accommodate panel pins to secure the device to the boards. We don't need to mark this out, just guess, but keep the holes inboard of the edge or the printed circuit board will split. Also, we don't need the centre punch for this operation, as that would split the board as well. Just press the drill bit lightly onto the surface and the drill will make its own mark in the soft copper surface.

3. The brass tube is no.#8121 from the K&S Metal Center range or ⅛in (3.18mm) diameter from the purveyors on eBay; K&S was £2.38 for two tubes 300mm long. The rod that will lock the deck and slide in the tube is 1.2mm diameter (89 pence for 300mm). The panel pins are 15mm long and one is shown at Fig. 75. It will need to be trimmed down to 10mm with the side-cutters or pliers before we can use it on the traverser deck section.

4. Figure 76 introduces another tool: the tube-cutter. Soft materials like brass, copper and aluminium would be destroyed if we tried to cut them with a hacksaw. The tube-cutter initially makes a score mark around the place to be cut and progressive tightening of the knurled hand wheel, at the bottom of the picture, will eventually result in the tube being parted. The steel blade that will do the cutting is just visible in the centre. This device is a K&S example but there are others on eBay for under £2. Make

Fig. 76   Cutting a tube.

sure it is a miniature tube-cutter, as there are plenty of plumber's examples that are used to cut 22mm and 15mm copper pipes, and they don't go down to the smaller sizes.

5. Figure 77 shows the preparation and assembly of the fixed parts of the locking mechanism. The copper-clad is first cleaned with either wire wool, emery board or any fine abrasive material, fluxed and then a blob of solder applied. I say blob, as to wait until the solder flows nicely might produce enough heat to separate the copper from the board. Use the rat-tail or needle file to hold the tube in position to solder it to the copper-clad. There is another use for the rat-tail file and that is to clean the end of the tube once it has been cut. The cutting process leaves a 'burr', which results in the tube diameter being reduced. We need to open it

Fig. 77   Fiddle yard loco track-locking catches – assembly.

Fig. 78 Fiddle yard loco track-locking catches – first fitting.

Fig. 79 Fiddle yard loco track-locking catches – wired up.

back out to the original diameter so that the 1.2mm brass rod will slide easily in and out. Try it out with a light piece of rolling stock over the track joint and do not push down but just push lightly. If all is well, secure the rest of the run-round track with track pins. The ends of these run-round tracks will need buffer stops but it is intended to place a backboard at the rear to avoid stock pitching off into the void.

6. The kit of parts is assembled on site (Fig. 78). First we trim the ends from a couple of sleepers and pin down the traverser deck part of the fixed mechanism with the two cut-down panel pins. Then slide in the 1.2mm brass rod, and slide the other part of the fixed mechanism onto the baseboard. The chipboard will happily

accept the 15mm panel pins. The 300mm piece of track needs a copper-clad sleeper at one end, drilled 1.25mm in two places. Secure the track in line with the traverser deck track and, if it is slightly out when viewed along the rails, tweak it into position with the soldering iron on the copper-clad sleeper. Bend up the brass rod at one end and cut so that the rod is just visible at the traverser deck end when the pin is fully engaged. Finally, when the tracks line up okay, solder the brass wire from the rail sides to the fixed mechanisms and take another cable from the black common cable we saw in Fig. 74. Test it with the largest locomotive you have, with the most wheels. The rail joint may appear rather large but as long as they line up both horizontally and vertically and the ends are chamfered, it'll run right. The Freightliner class 66 tries one of the run-round roads for size and it fits (Fig. 79). Repeat this for the other three tracks, but *see* step 7.

7. There is one variation to the run-round tracks. The fourth and last road does not line up with the incoming tracks at all. However, it may be useful to access a locomotive on this track if all others are occupied. As the fourth road is not lined up with the incoming tracks, it can't be fed power from there, as all the other tracks normally are. This means it has to be fed from the 300mm piece of track end but we need a means of controlling this as we don't want power there all the time if a loco is just parked.

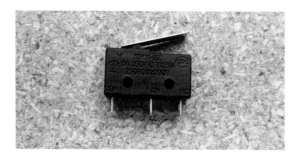

Fig. 80 Micro-switch.

Figure 80 is a gadget called a micro-switch. Although as switches go it is quite small, the term 'micro' refers to the action required to change it. They were originally introduced to limit the range of travel on an aircraft retractable undercarriage, where precision is paramount. They are now used in all manner of applications – in heating and ventilation, and the automotive industry. The device illustrated has three connections: the common, on the far left, and in the middle, the normally open contact, which means there is no circuit between common and this terminal until the lever is pressed. The far right is normally closed, which means there is a circuit between common and this one until the lever is pressed. In other words, this switch is a single pole changeover and can also be used to change point frog polarities, but not by us here.

The switch is incorrectly marked, which probably explains why a bag of ten of these items was £2.50 on eBay. They work perfectly well though.

Figure 81 shows the switch wired up for use on the fourth run-round road. The actual switching is with the black cable and the red is fed from one of the sliding bolts at the other end of the baseboard before it hits the traverser and so is permanently live, but the track is not powered until the switch is pressed. The locomotive can be driven out onto the traverser deck when the sliding catch is

Fig. 81 Micro-switch fitted to reverse power to the loco track.

connected and the switch pressed. When the loco reaches the traverser deck, you can let go of the switch as the deck has its own black cable. To shut off power to the traverser deck, simply side the catch to disconnect.

TRAVERSER DECK DEAD SECTIONS AND UNCOUPLER

The two furthest roads away from the operator were to house the DMUs of the passenger services from the two single-track branch lines, as they would not require any coupling services. The tracks are electrically split into two and could each accommodate a pair of 2-car sets, if required. Initially the intention was to use one 2-car and the class 153 single-car, but these intentions usually expand.

Figure 82 is a picture of the switches for these two roads. A piece of 0.8mm brass wire is secured using one of the small screws (please see Fig. 69)

Fig. 82 Isolating section switches made from brass wire.

Fig. 83 Fiddle yard uncoupling ramp.

from the sliding cupboard door packs that were not used on the deck lock. The other contact is a copper-clad sleeper soldered in and with a gap cut to avoid a short-circuit. The brass wire is connected with the same thinner brass wire we used for the run-round deck connectors. The hoop in the switch is to enable us to use a coffee stirrer, of the type issued in Costa or Starbucks, to operate the switch if the adjacent tracks are occupied and we want to move a train. The one further away is the prototype and the nearer one the production version.

Figure 83 is an uncoupling ramp made from the clear plastic sleeve you get with a Peco point. It is 1⅜in (35mm) long by ³⁄₁₀in (7mm) wide and secured by a pair of track pins that make the ramp appear about 3 or 4mm above rail height. One sleeve would provide possibly twenty ramps. The red marks by the sleepers are optimum positional indicators.

Figure 84 shows how we determine where those indicators are. The train is driven over the ramp so that the loco buffers are over the deck lock. Slowly reverse up and the vehicles will be uncoupled. Drive off to the run-round track. It is best to use empty vehicles as a test otherwise too high a ramp with a full vehicle would not be detected. An empty vehicle might be lifted off the track if the ramp were too high. Also the ramp needs to be right at the end of the deck. Repeat as required for the other three freight tracks. The class 57 uncoupling peg on the coupling appears to need to be longer as it only just clears the coupling bar on the wagon. We may need to superglue a small piece of brass wire to correct this but it does work.

The fiddle yard is almost complete mechanically but now needs its electrical systems to be designed and installed; and that will form part of the section on the control panel and wiring in Chapter 3. The traverser deck will need adjustments as it is used and the static parts of the sliding door locks will need two-part epoxy resin to glue them in place once you are happy it all works.

This fiddle yard piece has been a long description and readers, at this point, should be awarded a Long Service and Good Conduct medal, or possibly five minutes unfettered access to Hatton's warehouse for staying with it! However, much of it has been created from scratch to provide the fulcrum of operations for the layout, and much of the interest and fascination of how it will operate. It has been an exercise in providing the maximum facilities in the space available and yet could still be expanded further, if required.

Fig. 84 Class 57 uncoupling using ramp.

CHAPTER THREE

CONTROLLERS AND CONTROL

INTRODUCTION

The type of model railway controller is always a burning issue, but more than that is the way in which the layout is going to work like a real railway. This introduces the concept of interlocking, where a signal cannot be set to go until all the points on the route are suitably selected for that route. It goes further than that on single-track lines, of which we have two, in that no signal can be pulled off or set to go unless it is for the train travelling in the same direction for which the signal is allowing passage. This will require a brief overview of railway signalling and how it applies to this branch line, using both semaphore and colour light signals.

The relative merits of control systems are covered and then there is an individual study of each control component or sub-system.

ANALOGUE OR DIGITAL CONTROLLER

Analogue is where a DC voltage is applied to the track and a locomotive or train moves in direct response to the voltage being varied up and down. Trains can be isolated when not required with section switches or points that are set against the direction of travel.

Digital command control or DCC is where each locomotive or multiple unit is treated as an individually programmable device on tracks that are permanently live with an AC voltage. The alternating current is not true AC, as with a sine wave that would be generated at a power station, but pulsed, and within this mechanism is the ability to send out codes to first of all activate a specific locomotive and then to perform other functions.

DCC is marketed as a system that enables operators to control more than one locomotive on the track at once and the need for reduced inter-baseboard wiring. Perhaps the greatest single benefit is the dimension of sound where very accurate representations of the sound of working locomotives can be emitted by models either on the move or stationary.

Sound does come with a hefty price tag, doubling the price of most locomotives, and this layout is not one where the full benefits of multi-control of locomotives would be used. This feature is more suited to multiple-track main lines of a continuous run – 'the roundy roundy'. The operation of more than one locomotive at once on a layout of this type would be so fraught as to afford no fun in operation. In any case, the interlocking would rule such movements out.

In the 1950s, Trix Twin had a system where you could operate more than one train on one track at once. In the late 1970s, several companies introduced a forerunner to DCC, which, although there are devotees to this day, did not take off commercially.

With signals and ways of working to contend with, driving just one train properly in a prototype manner can be challenging. A DCC fault condition manifests itself as the entire system tripping out and nothing moving until the processor is rebooted.

The world is immeasurably a better place since the digital revolution, but not all activities benefit from it. So, on grounds of cost and layout type, it was decided to go for analogue control but to avoid the commercially available controllers for the following reasons.

Most DC controllers have operating characteristics that mean the controller cannot supply high power at low-speed settings. Unfortunately, this is exactly where the railways need high power – at slow speeds, to first of all overcome the inertia of a train weighing several hundred tonnes and then to keep it moving at slow speeds as it makes its way out of the freight yards or over the crossovers at some large station.

The answer to the problem is a stabilized variable power supply. What this has is the capacity to supply the maximum power at all voltage settings. They have short-circuit protection as standard and also have meters to tell us what voltage is supplied and how much current the locomotive is taking. This will help with running the locomotives day to day and is a management tool that will provide running and maintenance information. The units are also electrical test equipment and this will help us in diagnosing faults with point motors and testing LEDs used in the lighting.

The voltage is simply the electricity applied to the track. The current is a measure of the amount of power the locomotive is consuming. If the train is going up a gradient, the current will be more; and down a gradient, it will be less. The voltage will stay the same unless we change it.

The actual power supplied in a DC circuit is the voltage times current, but if the voltage is stabilized to a given value, then the current is proportional to the power that the model is taking. So a mechanism that is not running well can be detected by its higher current consumption and, if there is a problem with a locomotive mechanism, it will usually show on the ammeter. Also, when a value double that usually taken is shown, it may mean another loco is live on the layout somewhere else.

The only thing the stabilized power supply does not have for model railway use is a direction switch; this is simply a copy of the switches that have to be used for the point motors.

The direction changeover switch will be incorporated into the purpose-built control panel, which will be needed to control points and signals, and where the interlocking will take place electrically.

Another thing is that stabilized power supplies are cheaper but they do not have auxiliary supplies for points and signals and lighting. The stabilized power supply used is about half the price of a commercial controller but to which must be added auxiliary power supplies. However, this can be a good thing

as a short-circuit with the loco in an integrated power supply sometimes means the lights go dim or other services are affected.

Twelve-volt power supplies for points, signals and lights are cheaply available for external LED lighting and are to be found on eBay for less than £10. As an example, a 12V 4A unit retails for £6.25, including delivery, and 4A is way beyond that needed to power all the equipment in operation at once, which is not possible, as some of it will be interlocked out, always.

STABILIZED POWER SUPPLY CONTROLLER

The controller we shall be using at both station and fiddle yard ends is depicted in Fig. 85. It is described as 0–18V and while this is a little high for our

Fig. 85   Stabilized power supply as loco controller.

Fig. 86   Voltage and current class 66 running.

removed yet. In Fig. 85, a voltage of 3.13V has been selected but there is no loco connected to take any current. Voltage can be there on its own – current cannot be.

Now some inkling of what the controller can tell us about a locomotive that is running.

Figure 86 is the voltage needed, 3.09V, to just move the Freightliner class 66 on its own on level track, and when it is just moving, it takes 0.054A or 54mA.

In Fig. 87, with the same voltage applied, the wick has not been turned up, and the loco has met an immoveable object on the track and is stalled. The current is now 0.081A or 81mA. This is only a test and you are not advised to do this for a prolonged period as it may damage the motor, but you can now see how useful current indications are.

needs, commercial model railway controllers are only nominally 12V and can be higher. However, the current supply of 2A is more than enough for our needs. We could limit the current with the bottom knob but the unit is protected against short-circuit, as these items are designed to be used in test workshops and laboratories. The main control, then, is the voltage knob at the top; always ensure that the current control is turned fully to its maximum. The terminals accept standard 4mm plugs or bare wires. The 4mm plugs are often used to connect up loudspeakers, as well as for test purposes.

The backlit liquid crystal display is a little hazy but only because the protective film has not been

Fig. 87   Voltage and current class 66 stalled.

Fig. 88   Voltage and current class 153 running.

Fig. 89   Voltage and current class 57 running.

Figure 88 shows the Northern Rail class 153 just on the move at 2.64V but it takes 0.089A or 89mA running free. It may be that the lights take more current in the class 153 but it tells us all locomotives are not the same. (Note: after running-in, this loco now takes half the original current value.)

The start of movement of the Freightliner class 57 at 4.04V and 62mA is shown in Fig. 89. All these locomotives were bought second-user and it suggests to me that the class 57 is not as well run-in as the class 66 and has hardly been used. I would expect both those class 57 figures to fall with use.

The point is that all locomotives will differ slightly and by using the meters we will get to know and drive them differently as a result. Any fault will be readily apparent. The power supply was £47.73 with next-day timed delivery. All it needs is a direction-reversing switch and it will be good to go. The power supply/controller also comes in handy for checking point motors and such like before they are installed. For example, with the chosen point motor we have, we can expect one to take 50mA or 0.050A at 12V. These items are, after all, meant to be used in test laboratories and such.

AUXILIARY POWER SUPPLY

Figure 90 shows the 12V 4A fixed power supply for the point motors, signals and lights. It was £6.25 from eBay post-paid. If operation of the point motors causes lights to dim, then another will be purchased just for the lights. It will require us to wire this box up to the mains and that description

Fig. 90   12V 4.1A power supply.

Fig. 91   12V 4.1A power-supply connections.

follows. The power supply is CE marked, meaning it complies with European legislation and standards.

The business end of the power supply, as far as we are concerned, is shown in Fig. 91; there are five connections and their functions are as follows, from left to right:

1. Is AC Mains Live and we will connect a BROWN cable to this.
2. Is AC Mains Neutral and we will connect a BLUE cable to this.
3. Is the Earth and the cable is striped and GREEN.
4. Is the power output DC Negative and we need a BLACK or BLUE cable when we have installed this box.
5. Is the power output DC Positive and we need a RED cable when we have installed this box.

The further legend on the case on the far right refers to an adjustment for the output DC voltage. The voltage is adjusted, if need be, by the orange-coloured device on the right, which is called a potentiometer or, in techie-speak, a 'pot'. The pot is mounted on a copper-clad printed circuit board but we will not require it to provide us with any sleepers.

The most likely and easiest source of a mains cable to wire our power supply with is a cable to be found on a redundant piece of electrical equipment in the home. However, the following conditions must apply before we can do that:

- The cable must be in good condition, no kinks, chafing, splitting of the outer insulation, visible coloured cables or conductors.
- There must be no sign of overheating or burning and the plug must be in good condition with all three prongs present and a fuse of, ideally, 3A. Although the output is 4A DC, the input current is a fraction of that.
- The lead must have Live, Neutral and   rth inner cables. The two-cable type often found with 'phone chargers and lighter, non-earthed equipment is *not suitable*. The earth is a safety device for our protection with a metal-cased unit.

The lead must be at least 1m long, as it is to go from the control panel at baseboard height to floor level, so ideally would need to be 1.5–2m.

Using a Swann Morton scalpel, carefully remove the outer insulation layer from the cable and avoid damaging the mains conductor cables within. First draw the knife along the cable, starting about 5 cm from the end. Gripping it with your fingers, peel back the outer insulation and trim off with side-cutters, making sure there is no collateral damage

> **SAFETY TIP**
> Ensure that the mains lead is not plugged in before you start work.

Fig. 92   12V 4.1A power-supply mains connection 1.

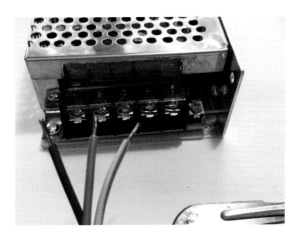

Fig. 93   12V 4.1A power-supply mains connection 2.

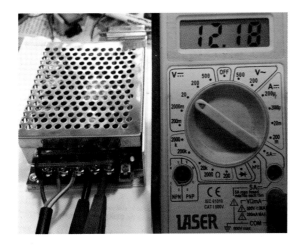

Fig. 94   12V 4.1A power-supply mains connection 3, checking output.

to the coloured cables inside (Fig. 92). If there is, have another go and start from fresh.

For each coloured conductor, strip off about 6–8mm to reveal the copper conductors, ensuring that you have not cut through the copper and lost any. Twist the conductors in the fingers to ready them for insertion into the terminal block (Fig. 93).

If the cable is not ready to connect, as shown at this point, simply cut the whole piece off and start again (and at this point, the original selection of a 2m cable seems a wise choice).

Flip up the plastic terminal cover lid and connect the cables, as previously described, using a cross-point screwdriver *but don't plug in yet*. Ensure there are no stray conductor wires anywhere. Not all these power supplies feature the plastic lid.

Connect an electrical test meter (the type shown is currently on eBay for £3.20). The black cable goes to terminal 4 and the red to terminal 5. Select DC voltage, as shown: the solid and dotted lines represent DC values and the range we require is '20'. In other words, any DC voltage up to a maximum of 20V would be measured. If we had selected the wrong scale, for example, if the voltage was actually 50 and we had selected 20, the meter just flashes at you in annoyance. Close the orange terminal cover.

Plug our newly configured, checked and fused mains cable into a mains socket and switch on.

The result should be as shown in Fig. 94 – 12.18V DC is fine and we do not need to adjust the 'pot', although if it was not 12V or thereabouts, a small cross-point screwdriver would be needed to make adjustments.

The green light-emitting diode (LED) simply shows that the mains is connected and switched on. If a short-circuit occurs, the green LED is extinguished and power is cut off until the short-circuit is removed.

If you don't have any redundant mains cable about, then you will need to buy 6½ft (2m) of 5A three-core mains cable for £4.99 from eBay, plus a plug with 3A fuse for £1.55. You will need to wire the plug in accordance with the plug's instructions (for further information: http://en.wikipedia.org/wiki/AC_power_plugs_and_sockets_-_British_

and_related_types). Ensure that the cable clamp is in use and correctly positioned on the outer sheath.

Switch off the mains and remove the plug. The unit is now ready for installation when the control panel is built. When it is installed, always connect the DC cables first before plugging in and switching on.

POINT MOTORS

As already stated, the decision was taken to use Fulgurex slow-acting point motors, as it was felt they are easier to mount and the amount of baseboard hacking about is kept to a minimum. They provide a device to transmit movement from the underside of the baseboard to the point tie-bar and they can usually be fixed if there is a problem.

Fulgurex are a Swiss outfit and are well known in larger gauge modelling circles as manufacturers of precision live steam and electric locomotives. They also manufacture model cars.

Fig. 96   Fulgurex point motor and actuating rod.

Fig. 95   Fulgurex point motor as bought.

The motor arrives in a blister pack and, as it says on the reverse, the blister pack can be used as a dust cover after installation (Fig. 95). Carefully remove the blister with the Swann Morton scalpel and retain for future use. The dust cover will need to be modified but we won't know how until the motor has been installed.

Figure 96 shows the Fulgurex point motor before installation. The two shiny connectors on the lower right-hand side are the 12V DC input and the motor is driven first this way and then reversed by reversing the polarity of the DC supply. The point actuating shaft runs north to south and vice versa through the geared motor. The shaft has the two holes in either end for the brass wire. There are two pillars attached to the shaft and their purpose is to switch off the motor when it has reached its limit of travel in either direction. The DC polarity is sensed by two diodes underneath the black mounting plate, which are a one-way street for current flow.

The micro-switches are in two banks of two: the bottom switches control the motor and the top two in both cases are free for other uses. One of the switches can be used for the point frog but we shall use another relay for extra reliability. All switches are of the changeover type, as we saw on the micro-switch on the run-round track.

In this case, we shall retain the spare micro-switches as spares for the main motor switches. They should operate reliably for some years as they are, if properly installed, but belt and braces never come amiss where functions are critical. The motor is shown in the mid-position, which is the position they recommend for installation. Basically, the point blades are set to their mid-position during installation and the throw of the point motor should be enough to drive the point blades to their limit in either direction and any excess movement from the motor creates a spring effect on the Z-shaped piece of brass, which effectively locks the blades in position. Not exactly a facing point locking mechanism as such but the nearest we'll get to it in model form in this scale. Below-board solenoid point motors do not act as positively as this.

The operating arm, depicted on the right in Fig. 96, will need to be modified. For this you will need a tube-cutter and needle file to reduce its length. In addition, the brass insert wire will be bent into a Z-shape so that the movement can be transmitted through the baseboard. Both of the latter tasks can only be done at installation.

Figure 97 is a view of one side of the Fulgurex point motor and it is useful to let us see the contact arrangement. The bottom set of contacts at both ends of the motor travel on the blue terminal blocks are for motor control and you can just see the connections coming out of the black base to them. It would be a simple matter to use the upper contacts should the bottom set finally give up the ghost.

Fig. 98 *Fulgurex point motor ready to fit.*

However, you may wish to use the upper contacts for frog control and it would not matter which set you used, the centre contact is always the frog itself and the outer pair, the toe of the stock rails. The actual way round these go is trial and error when making the connection. You could sit and work it out, but by the time you've done that you could have finished the job. The micro-switches appear to have been modified in recent years and seem more reliable. However, experience shows these motors can operate for years without mishap.

Figure 98 shows the Fulgurex point motor prepared for use. There are four mounting-screw holes altogether, one in each corner. Only two are used and they are in the same plane as the motor slide mechanism. Any slight bend in the baseboard can cause the black north–south slider to stick or lock up. So, using screw holes that would make this worse is avoided and instead two screw holes in line with the slider are chosen. The two holes on the right are too close to the micro-switches, so it is the two on the left that are chosen, and they are countersunk to accept the screws, as shown.

The motor has been tested in both directions with the loco power supply or controller we saw in Fig. 85. The motor takes about 50mA or 0.050A at 12V, as it should. It takes nothing when stationary. The motor needs to be actuated to the mid-position again before fitting.

Finally, solder one cable to each main tag and terminate the cables in a piece of 'chocolate strip', so-called because the connecting strip comes in

Fig. 97 *Fulgurex point motor and micro-switch connections.*

chunks about six times the size shown and pieces are cut or broken off as you might with a chocolate bar. A chunk of strip is £0.32 from Toolstation, at present. Anything that can be used for the railway electrically that are general-use electrical items, are an order of magnitude cheaper at either Toolstation or Screwfix.

The purpose of the chocolate strip is that it allows us to install the motor and not worry about which way round the DC polarity is. The switch on the control panel will indicate, by its position, which way the point motor is to move and clearly the point motor must move in concert with the selection we have made. The chocolate strip just lets us make a mistake and then reconnect if we are wrong. In addition, it avoids a soldered joint being made underneath the baseboards and, should we ever need to remove the motor, it is easily done in seconds without a soldering iron.

At this point, if you prefer to use the spare micro-switch on the point motor to switch the frog, the point motor is now ready to use when the frog cables are connected to the micro-switch. The frog must be the centre cable.

However, if a relay is to be used, then we carry on as instructed here. We will definitely need relays when we interlock points and signals, and relays abound on the prototype railways with special buildings built to house them.

Figure 99 shows the up side of a relay acquired from eBay in a job lot of fifty for less than £10, post-paid from China, which is where most of this stuff is made. You have to wait a couple of weeks whilst the item languishes in customs, but you can antici-pate any requirement to arrive just when you need

it by a bit of planning. Very often equipment is sold off at the end of a construction phase in a factory and they ask not much more than it cost to make to get rid of it.

A relay consists of a coil that, by electromagnetic action, changes over at least one set of contacts that are controlling a separate circuit. The most popular arrangement is one common connection, which has one contact connected to one contact with no power applied to the coil and a different contact connected with power applied. These contacts are usually referred to as NC, normally closed, and NO, normally open, where 'normal' means with no coil power applied. This is exactly what we need for frog switching.

This is the same concept as the micro-switch we used on the run-round traverser track, except that the labelling was wrong. It must be incredibly dif-ficult for someone in China used to an alphabet of 4,000 characters to adapt to just 26 and vice versa, and particularly when those characters have no resemblance whatsoever to each other.

It tells us that the relay coil is 12V and that is the most important bit. The rest of it tells us that the contacts will handle mains voltage of up to 10A, less if the AC circuits are heavily inductive, which is remarkable with a device that is only about 25mm long. However, we will only be using loco voltage and current for frog switching, which, as we have seen, is around a few volts and less than 100mA or 0.1A. As the relay is only passing very low current and it is hermetically sealed, it should last for many years.

Figure100 shows the flip side and where the con-nections are to be made. On the right-hand side are

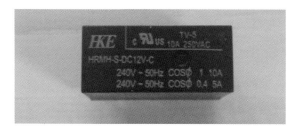

Fig. 99   Point frog relay.

Fig. 100   Point frog relay connections.

the 12V DC connections for the relay coil and to the left, the changeover contacts. The top contact is common and as can just be seen on the diagram on the switch is connected normally to the bottom right of the trio – NC. The other contact is the NO contact and this is made when the coil is energized.

Figure 101 is a diagrammatic representation

of a relay and its operation, and whilst individual construction details may vary, the principle of operation is the same. Where it says 'either polarity' it means that it does not matter how you connect the positive and negative DC wires, it still works just the same.

Figure 102 introduces the concept of the diode or one-way street for electric current. We have already mentioned these in terms of Fulgurex point motor control, but as we are to use these in the frog change-over relay, and point and signal interlocking, it is essential we know how they work and how to connect them up.

The top of the image is a diagram of a typical commercially available diode, the 1N4001, and a 'bandolier' of 100 diodes will set you back £1.69 post-paid from eBay at present. Why buy less or pay more? The 1N4001 type passes a maximum 'forward' current of 1A and the semiconductor will tolerate up to 50V before it irretrievably breaks down.

As the current we shall pass will be about 50mA, this is the same as 0.050A, so well within the design criteria for the diode. The voltage we are using is also well within design limits.

There are other diodes that will tolerate mains voltages and are used in the conversion of AC to DC, known as rectification.

The silver band around one end of the diode

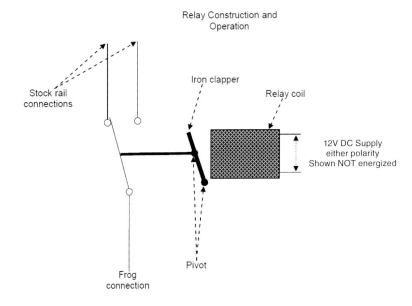

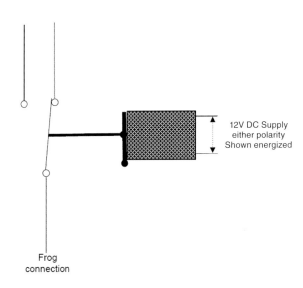

Fig. 101   Relay construction and operation.

denotes the polarity that will accept or reject current flow. The diagrammatic version in the middle uses a similar idea.

The LED version at the bottom in Fig. 102 also blocks current in one direction, but when the current does flow, it emits light and the colour of the light is dependent on the materials used in the semiconductor wafer when it was being made. LEDs are almost everywhere and we shall be using some for indication purposes on the control panel.

Figure 103 is the complete sub-assembly for the point motor and frog switching. It incorporates an 1N4001, which is just peeping out from the two-way chocolate block. This is because if it was not there, the relay would operate whenever the point motor was energized and, as we've already seen, one of the frog switches relies on the relay being de-energized at some point. In other words, without a diode, the same rail of the point would always be live and so there would be a short-circuit on one selection when locomotive power was applied.

The relay supplies the two rails at the toe of the point and yellow is the frog, wired from the three-way chocolate block.

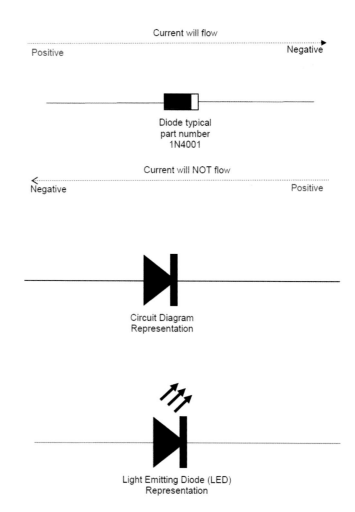

Fig. 102   *Diode operation and symbolism.*

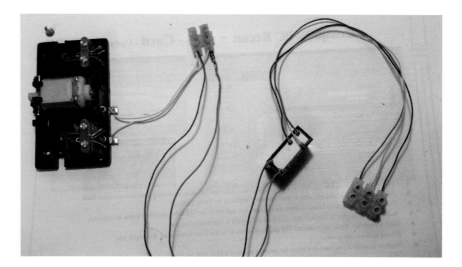

Fig. 103   Point motor and frog-changing relay kit ready to fit.

The operation of the circuit is as follows:

1. Let's suppose 12V DC is applied to the two-way chocolate block, and positive is on the right and negative is on the left. The point motor runs to its end-stop and the diode does not oppose current flow and the relay is operated. The frog changes over.

2. Flip the switch on the control panel and reverse the polarity and this time the motor runs to the opposite end-stop but the diode blocks current flow in that circuit and the relay does not operate, and the opposite rail is connected to the frog.

Of course, which rail is which and which way round the motor operates on the control panel for the selection and frog changeover is a local negotiation; this is why it is all connected by a chocolate block, so that any of it can be swapped round, except the frog yellow cable, when installing the motor.

The cabling used is the only component not so far mentioned and that will be coming up shortly.

SEMAPHORE SIGNAL MOTORS

The layout is designed to have a mixture of semaphore signals in the station area and colour light signals beyond. This is still common practice in various parts of the country – there are about 500 mechanical signal boxes with semaphore signalling on Network Rail in the summer of 2015.

Whereas the point motor is quite involved and complicated because of frog switching, signal motors are the opposite.

The solenoid is another electrical device that is all around us. Some types of car starter-motor have a solenoid to engage the gear on the engine flywheel to crank the engine over on start-up. When power to the starter motor is switched off, the solenoid disengages from the engine flywheel, otherwise the starter motor would then be driven by the car engine.

Lower current solenoids are to be found in access control systems where a device typically operates a door lock.

Figure 104 illustrates the basis of the semaphore signal motor. The solenoids depicted come from eBay and a dealer in Hong Kong, and they were £21.60 for twelve post-paid. They are 12V and take 0.085A or 85mA.

The base shown in Fig 105 is aluminium and is from the scrap box, but almost any rigid, easily cut material will do. If you desire aluminium, then it is £7.99 for 600mm × 25mm × 1.5mm from eBay. Pieces 80mm-long are then cut off with the hacksaw and 3.5mm-holes drilled for the securing screws and the brass rod through the middle. The coil is secured with 5-minute two-part epoxy resin from the Pound Shop.

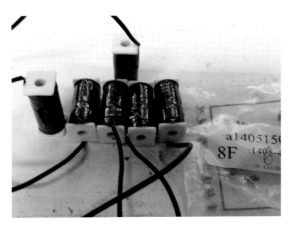

Fig. 104 *Signal motor solenoid coils as bought.*

Fig. 105 *Signal motor base in production.*

The solenoids as bought do not come with the bit in the middle that moves, and here it is essential that the steel in the middle is a sloppy fit. This is because when the coil is energized, if it is a loose fit, it is suspended in mid-air by the magnetic field but oscillates up and down before stabilizing in position. This imparts mechanical bounce to the signal arm, which is most realistic. The steel rod used is described as 'bright mild steel' and is £3.20 for 300mm and 3.18mm diameter, although most of the merchants on eBay still use Imperial units, which translates to 12in long by ³⁄₁₆in diameter in old money.

Into the mild steel rod is inserted the 0.8mm brass rod, after a 1mm-hole has been drilled in the top of the rod. This is quite tricky – the rod will need to be held in the vice and the drill rotated slowly until it gets a good start; WD-40 is good as a lubricant. The wire is then soldered into the top of the steel with plenty of flux and heat.

Figure 106 illustrates a finished example ready for installation. The motor part of it is another 'gizmo' that shares some similarities with relays but, instead of changing over contacts, it imparts movement to a piece of iron that can be magnetized when the circuit is energized.

The action of the motor is very simple and the motor is mounted beneath the baseboards with a pair of 10mm no.8 screws. A hole is drilled in the baseboard to allow the brass wire to protrude and connect to the signal mechanism.

The crucial part is the length of the steel rod and where it is mounted when installed. About 1½in (40mm) long is the maximum and the steel rod must be at the position shown, just intruding into the solenoid body for it to work effectively. Too far away from the solenoid coil body and the steel won't be attracted; too far into the body and there won't be enough movement to move the signal arm. If the steel body is too long, it won't be attracted in the optimum position – saw a bit off the bottom until it works. You can play around with this using the loco power supply set to 12V and mark off the optimum setting with a felt-tipped pen on the steel. Make sure the motor is vertical when you do this. This is trial and error, and depends upon what type

Fig. 106   Signal motor with armature.

of solenoid you have, but once you've done one, the rest follow the same pattern. Once this issue is resolved, the brass wire can be trimmed and fitted to the signal arm.

The application of 12V to the coil makes the steel move upwards and this pulls the signal arm 'off' or to the 'go' position. Remove power and the signal returns to danger or 'on' under gravity. This has the benefit of a 'fail safe' feature, which is how real signals work. Five signals powered, realistically, will cost about £4 each if you use the bought aluminium, and about £2.50 each if you use recycled base material.

CABLES AND CONNECTORS

None of the above equipment will work unless we can hook it up and connect it all together. The connectors are used to connect control panels to baseboards at both ends of the layout and to connect the station control panel to the fiddle yard by a separate cable. The connectors and cables can be made up in 'looms' on the workbench. They are then fitted and finally connected up to the equipment on the baseboards and control panels. This use of connectors will ensure portability of the layout and it is a much easier proposition to expand the layout electrically when this concept is adopted.

CONNECTORS

The connector chosen was the 25-way 'D-range' or D-type. These are so named in that the connector body is vaguely D-shaped and this acts as a kind of keyway to ensure that two connectors are not mis-connected. In addition, the pins for the connectors are arranged in two rows: one of thirteen pins and the other of twelve. This feature also makes it impossible to connect these items the wrong way round. If the device had been circular with symmetrically arranged pins, it might have been possible to get the pins out of 'sync' and mis-connect the device.

The connectors were widely used in computers up until the late 1990s, and were used for connecting devices that used serial communications. The serial communication standard was referred to as RS232 and the connectors are often sold as such.

RS232 was overtaken by the universal serial bus or USB; personal computers started to use this from about 1997. However, the up-side, as far as model railways are concerned, is that there is much RS232-related equipment on the market and, as factories making PCs and anything with the need for a serial interface are no longer there, the RS232 equipment is quite good value and a fraction of the price it once was. There is a subset of RS232 that was widely used in laptops and consists of only nine pins.

Connectors consist of a connector body with either pins or sockets moulded into an insulating base. When all the pins and sockets have been soldered in position, a shroud is clipped into place and this has the job of 'strain relief' on the cables, exactly as we have in a mains plug. This is essential if the connectors are to tolerate connection and disconnection without pulling individual cables out from their sockets.

Gender-specificity and expressing one gender in terms of another has been avoided in the book so far but connector terminology does employ gender-specific references – but only for illustrative purposes and not to cause offence to anyone. Connectors with pins are referred to universally as 'male' and those with sockets as 'female'. This

Fig. 107 RS232 D-type 25-way connectors.

is important, not least when buying or ordering equipment, as the connector types will usually be expressed in those terms.

Figure 107 shows a pair of D-type 25-way connectors, male and female; both have the black shroud fitted and they are compatible, even though from different manufacturers. The connector body on the left has some of the connections wired

A pair of male and female D-type connectors are about £2 post-paid from eBay and a pair of shrouds are similarly priced. They are suitable for low voltages only and 12V DC is ideal, but mains voltages were never designed to be used with such connectors.

CABLE

The cable used is eight-core alarm cable and from Screwfix it is £24.36 for a 100m drum (Fig. 108). The cable comes plastic-sheathed and when the sheath

Fig. 108 Eight-core alarm wire.

is stripped away, the individual cables within make admirable loose connector wire of the sort we saw in Fig. 103 to wire up the point motor assemblies. The cable insulation will withstand a voltage of up to 50V DC and a current of 1A, continuous rating. The maximum voltage we are using is 12V nominal and in the range 10–18V. The maximum current would be a point motor plus relay, which equals 85mA or 0.085A and that is not continuous, so well within the cable's capacity.

Even if we operated four point-motors at once, which would be the maximum possible on the station layout, that would only be 0.34A and that would only be for a few seconds and spread across several cables anyway.

That 800m of cable for £24.36 works out at a little over 3 pence a metre, whereas that sold as model railway wire is about 20 pence per metre. Although some of it is rated at 1.4A and more, we don't need that extra current carrying capacity. In any case, much thicker wire will mean it is more difficult to wire up the connectors.

WIRING THE LOOMS

The connectors are capable of handling twenty-five cables and three times eight of the alarm cable is twenty-four, and so there are three groups of eight cables. Individual alarm cables are denoted as 'A', 'B' or 'C' to help identify the cables within.

Fig. 109   Preparing to connect alarm wire to RS232 25-way connector.

Fig. 110   Connections where top-left is pin 1.

The alarm cable has been carefully stripped back about 2in (50mm) so that we can strip the individual cable ends in preparation for the soldering to the connector (Fig. 109). We only need about 3mm to solder into the connector cups but it is easier if you strip a little more and trim to size after the conductors have been tinned. The cable size is 24 American Wire Gauge (AWG) if you are using wire strippers (eBay £4.98 post-paid). Wire strippers do speed the job up if you have 200-plus wires of the same diameter to strip.

Twist the conductors and dunk in the flux and tin with the soldering iron. Then trim to a length of about 3mm.

Mount the connector by its steel edge, NOT by its body, into a vice or clamp. Wipe the connector cups with flux and place the wire in the cup. Apply heat to the rear of the cup for about 2sec until the solder melts, then remove the iron and allow cooling.

The connector shown in Fig. 110 is **female** and the pins run, from left to right, top row, 1 to 13. Bottom row left to right is 14 to 25 *viewed from the rear.*

A male connector is 180 degrees out of phase (!) and the pins run, from right to left, top row, 1 to 13. Bottom row right to left is 14 to 25 *viewed from the rear.*

They are marked on the white insulator front and rear but it is quite difficult to spot and you need good light to see it.

In Fig. 110, the first eight-core cable colours run as follows:

1. RED
2. BLACK
3. ORANGE
4. BLUE
5. BROWN
6. GREEN
7. YELLOW
8. WHITE

The system repeats itself using the same colour ordering for the next two eight-core cables and the sixteen cores within. Therefore we always know that red is either number 1, 9 or 17 in any connector and that brown is always 5, 13 or 21, and so on.

Note that you need good light for this, as with indifferent light, brown closely resembles black.

Figure 111 is a connector in the process of being wired up for three cable groups and pin 25 is the last and is shown not populated. Note the piece of card from the Fulgurex packet that just separates and insulates the rows of conductors from each other. In a factory environment, each coloured cable would have its own rubber sleeve covering the conductor and connector cup.

Figure 112 is the final stage of wiring the 25-way connector and the red sleeve is heat shrink tubing, which has the unusual property of reducing its

Fig. 112   RS232 connector almost ready to fit.

diameter when heated and thus forming a tight durable protection for cables. This is available from eBay in a variety of diameters and colours as a pack of assorted lengths – the cost is about £2 to £5. You would also need a heat source. A hot-air paint-stripper is effective but do remove the heat as soon as the tube shrinks. A hairdryer does not generate enough heat. Gas torches are available but a naked flame is not recommended. Alternatively, you can use self-adhesive electrical tape to bind round the three white-sheathed cables.

The purpose of either the heat shrink or tape is to provide a base to which to clamp the cables, to avoid damage and to hold the cables firmly so there is no possibility of them being pulled apart and connections lost.

The shroud is held in position by the cable clamps at the bottom of the connector and the black plastic cover clips into position. The long, steel screws are not really needed here as they are used for securing into a panel but are shown here to illustrate the complete assembly. These connectors will be free-range in that sense.

CONTROL PANEL

There were two control panels constructed for the station board and the fiddle yard. Their construction was identical in the sense of the timber frame

Fig. 111   Completed connections of three cable groups of eight cables.

and aluminium panel but, naturally, their control facilities are quite different.

The drawing (Fig. 113) consists of three parts and for now we are just looking at the top part entitled 'Control panel framework'. The framework is basically a rectangle into which will fit an aluminium panel bought pre-cut on eBay and the circuit specialist stabilized power supply, which we are using

Fig. 114   *Control panel first steps.*

as a controller. As it has an ammeter, we can also use it to test point and signal motors too, but more of that later.

The trestle support is used to bolster the framework and, as the control panel is to be bolted to the baseboards, it is the logical place to mount the framework. It is also ergonomically suitable for an operator and right-handed people can still operate the controls left-handed.

The framework is part-assembled using the same 75mm decking screws that were used to secure the blocks underneath the baseboards (Fig. 114). The embryo framework is held in place by a G-clamp, whilst suitable 3mm pilot holes are drilled, which can just be seen. These holes are then widened out to 8mm to accept M8 coach bolts that will hold the completed framework and power supply securely to the baseboards. The coach bolts are about £2.50 for ten in the zinc-plated version. There is a Rolls Royce solution of stainless steel but there is also a budget. In any case, if we have to trim these to length, the frame hacksaw will make short work of zinc-plated but a big deal with stainless steel, which is a much harder metal.

Figure 115 is the fiddle yard end and this time we have to take account of the traverser deck before drilling the pilot and 8mm holes. The M8 coach bolts are seen fitted in this view and as coach bolts are usually supplied in a minimum of 100mm lengths, they are a wee bit too long – 75mm is plenty long

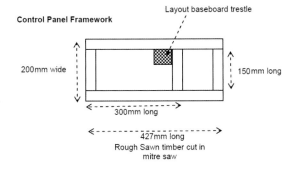

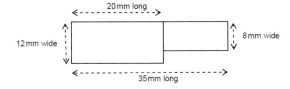

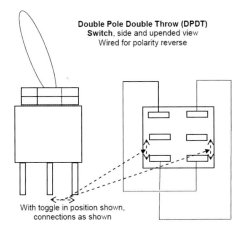

Fig. 113   *Control panel drawings.*

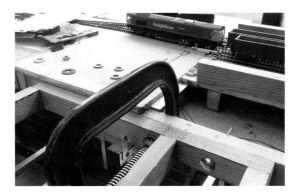

Fig. 115   Fiddle yard control panel first steps.

Fig. 117   Station control panel with power supply fitted.

enough, as they have to go through two lots of 25mm-thick framing and still leave enough to get the nut and washer on. The coach bolts have the large circular head that acts as a washer to avoid crushing the wood and a square locating piece behind the head, which digs into the wood. This makes it easier to remove the control panel and refit if the bolt is to some extent captive. Make sure that any coach bolts purchased have no more than 50mm of blank shaft that does not have a screw thread on it.

When the coach bolt is to be trimmed, fit the nut first and mark off the 75mm with a felt-tipped pen. Hold the head of the bolt in a vice and saw off the unwanted piece. Then clean up the saw cut with a file and unscrew the nut, which will act as a guide as to whether the screw thread is usable. Too stiff and the file needs more work.

Fig. 116   Station control panel ready to receive power supply.

The process of completion of the frame can begin once the framework is secured to the baseboard (Fig. 116). The rear piece is then dismantled to enable the power supply to be fitted.

The power supply is held in position by two of its feet, but we need the chock at the front to make the power supply sit up in the position shown (Fig. 117). The chock is detailed on the second part of Fig. 113, and is made from scrap wood. As its name suggests, it is not secured by glue or any other means and this will enable the power supply to be removed easily to use elsewhere, if required.

Figure 118 depicts the addition of the 8in by 12in by $\frac{1}{16}$in (300mm by 200mm by 1.5mm thick) aluminium plate that we will use to hold all the control panel switches for points' signals, lights and track power. (The aluminium plates cost £6.50 from eBay for two pieces cut to size and delivered.) Aluminium is still reasonably cheap, but is easily drilled and worked. It is also easily damaged and is supplied with a plastic film over the metal on one side. This plastic film is useful in that we can draw out the plan of what will be drilled where.

The 25mm-framework outlined by felt-tipped pen is simply a reminder that we can't drill within that boundary, as that is where the wooden framework is and the body of a switch would intrude in such a position. The track plan is sketched out and suitable drilling holes marked out, mindful of the dimensions of the switches we must fit. The double-slip will need LEDs to show us which tracks are selected. There are section switches too where locomotives can be isolated independent of the fact that the points will isolate them as well.

The power supply now has a double-pole double-throw (DPDT) switch mounted in position and this addition makes the power supply a controller (Fig. 119).

The final part of the diagram on Fig. 113 shows the wiring needed before we install the switch and we can see the positive and negative cables from the controller to the DPDT switch. The connections needed are the centre pair and one other pair.

This wiring is needed for all the point motors

as well, as they operate on the DC power supply reversal principle. With the two controllers and seven point motors and a further power changeover switch needed in the fiddle yard, this is a total of ten switches that need this wiring treatment. There are only seven switches for effectively eight points, as the loco release crossover will only use one switch.

Before we get into the installation and wiring phase of the layout, it is necessary to describe the way it will work in terms of traffic flows and what facilities are needed to service it. This will directly affect the installation and equipment needed to get it to work.

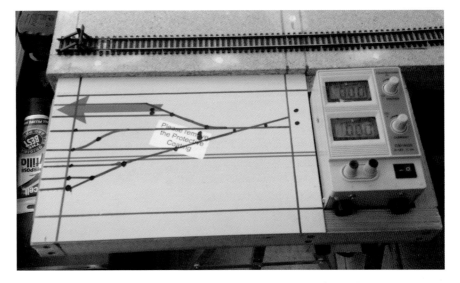

Fig. 118   Station control panel with aluminium sheet offered up.

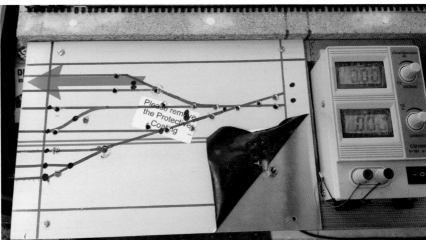

Fig. 119   Station control panel with aluminium sheet drilled for controller direction switch.

CHAPTER FOUR

WAY OF OPERATING AND TRAFFIC FLOWS

INTRODUCTION

The prototype was chosen to be around Buxton because of the traffic flows that are there today. We cannot model an actual location because they are all too big to fit in the available space when scaled down to model size. However, what we do model must be plausible to be believable. Buxton has two single track branch lines but no passenger service on these lines, which we have at the fictional Dovedale to generate more traffic and interest.

TRAFFIC FLOWS

Figure 120 is a schematic diagram of the Network Rail tracks around Buxton, in Derbyshire, and beyond. The thick black lines are double-track and the thinner lines single-track. The dotted line is single-track to our imaginary, yet plausible, terminus of Dovedale. The black circles are actual mechanical signal boxes in 2015 and the blue circle our rendition of Dovedale Station.

Such a place exists but never had a railway. It is in a beautiful part of the country and attracts a million visitors every year. As so often in Derbyshire, the scenery has to co-exist with extensive limestone quarrying, which adds to the traffic flows. Such as it is, this is all perfectly plausible, although perhaps a business case for the railway might struggle. Happily we are only concerned with the business case for the model version and some licence has been used as to the actual location of Dovedale. Our Dovedale had a four-platform terminus station in the 1960s but that has been cut back to a single, island platform, although some remnants of the former layout remain, Chinley Junction for real had six platforms and now has two. The plat-

form at Dovedale itself has been truncated from one capable of holding a six-coach train to a 2-car DMU length. This is a common enough scenario on Network Rail. There is a station named Dove Holes, which refers to caves in the Dove Valley; it is tolerably close to our location but on the Manchester to Buxton route.

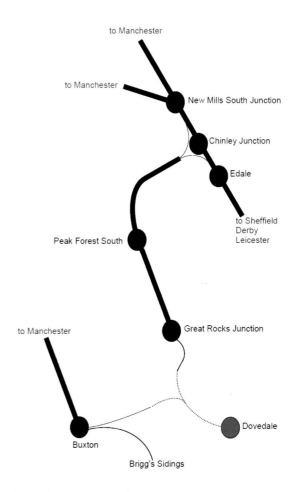

Fig. 120 Dovedale – fact and fiction.

Fig. 121 Llandudno Junction Station, class 158 in the bay platform.

Figure 121 is a picture of a class 158 waiting to depart from Llandudno Junction Station for Llandudno on the North Wales Coast line. The platform next to it was taken out of use and the track removed in the 1970s.

Attractive parts of the country attract people to go and live there and Dovedale has thriving commuter traffic to Buxton for Manchester, and Chinley Junction for Sheffield and beyond. The two services connect at Dovedale. The former is a single-car class 153 and the latter a two-car class 158. In addition, there is regular traffic conveying visitors to the town.

Some of the substantial limestone traffic from the quarries in the area has to reverse at Dovedale, much as they now do at Buxton for real. In fact, some limestone trains, due to the nature of the track layout, have to run round twice in a short distance of 5 miles (8km).

Back to the model now and some of the loaded trains come from the Chinley Junction direction, from the quarries at Peak Forest South and Great Rocks Junction, reverse at Dovedale and then head off to Buxton and Manchester, which is a considerably shorter journey than going by Chinley Junction. In any case, there are not enough paths for freight trains on the Chinley route – a situation reflected on many routes on Network Rail.

Empties returning to the quarries take the reverse route. The capacity of the run-round facility at Dovedale and the fiddle yard is three bogie hopper wagons. It would be nice if there were twenty hopper wagons, as some prototype trains are, but that would require the run-round facilities to be 25ft (7.62m) long, which is twice the length of the entire layout. However, there are stone-carrying trains from Mountsorrel in Leicestershire in 2015 that are as short as two bogie hoppers and a few four-wheel wagons.

The train operating companies involved are Northern Rail for the passenger services and Freightliner for the stone traffic with DB Schenker, another major player, for motive power in the area, as it is in real life.

Figure 122 shows a pair of class 150 2-car DMUs at Buxton Station, which, although it has two platforms, only really uses the platform nearer the camera, platform 2; the far platform 1 is for stock storage. When the time comes for the unit further away to occupy the nearer platform, it does so, but the signalling can accept a further train to occupy platform 2, even though it is already occupied by another DMU. This is quite a rare working at smaller stations, although it is often seen at larger stations where platforms are divided up into A, B and so on.

Fig. 122 Buxton Station, class 150s occupy platforms.

Note the red stop lamps at the driver's eye line – we will return to these later in the construction phase.

Figure 123 is a picture of Freightliner class 66, 66 613 leaving the cement factory at Tunstead, Great Rocks Junction with a train of Lafarge cement. Note the smaller subsidiary armed semaphore signal to let the train out onto the main line.

Fig. 123 Great Rocks Junction and class 66 departs with Lafarge cement train.

Fig. 124   Class 66 with Lafarge cement train heads for Peak Forest South.

Figure 124 and the Lafarge cement train is out on the main line now from the cement works and heading towards Peak Forest South with 66 613 at its head. Note the DB Schenker class 60 at the top of the gradient and the recently shunted limestone hoppers on the far right. The DB Schenker class 66 that was doing the shunting has sped off leaving the hoppers on their own until the train engine is backed on. This is a typical class 66 shunt with loaded hopper wagons, as the class 08 that used to do the work did not possess the capacity to achieve acceptable brake pressure quickly enough. DB Schenker put most of its fleet of class 08 and 09 locomotives up for sale as a result in May 2015, although 08 shunters were still at work in Eastleigh track maintenance yards in July 2015.

WAYS OF WORKING

ABSOLUTE BLOCK

Originally, prior to the 1880s, there was the time-interval system, which meant you could dispatch a train some minutes after the passage of another. This was all well and good until the original train was stopped for some reason or traffic densities and speeds increased. There were some horrific accidents with this system, or lack of it.

A concept used almost since railways began is the 'block' of track where a train is permitted to move from block to block of track, provided no other train was in the block. This relies on there being up and down double tracks. This block system was worked by block instruments that conveyed the track occupancy status and by a bell system that was used to communicate with adjacent signal boxes.

If you look at Fig. 125, it shows two British Rail absolute block instruments. At the bottom of each instrument is the block bell. There are two instruments, as the signal boxes either side both have to be communicated with – a terminus only has one. The two signal boxes in question are at Sudbury and Tutbury in Staffordshire on the Stoke to Derby line. The actual signal box in which this equipment is housed is Scropton Crossing.

The default condition for the section of track is described as Normal, which means the same as Line Blocked. In other words, no permissions have been granted for any movement.

Fig. 125 Scropton signal box block instruments and diagram.

The sector to the right coloured green is Line Clear.

The sector to the left is Train on Line and that is coloured red.

The reason for the two dials is because the signal box that is receiving the train has to make the selections of Line Clear and Train on Line but any selection must be mirrored in the other signal box and vice versa, so that both signallers are aware.

In Fig. 126, there is a representation, at a most basic level, of the structure of a block section.

Network Rail's actual locations may be different for mainly operational reasons and there may well be more signals in the sections at busier parts of the railway.

The red signals are called 'home' signals and they are stop or go. Stop is termed ON and go is termed OFF. The yellow signal is a distant signal and is a function of a train's weight and speed in that it might take a mile (1.6km) to stop a heavy train that is going fast. The distant signal gives the driver a warning that the next signal will be stop if the signal

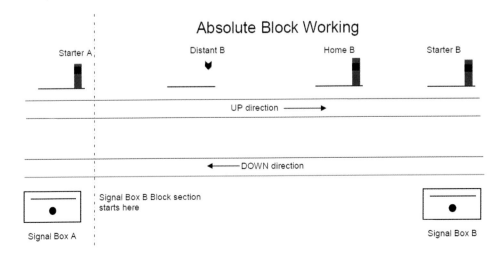

Fig. 126 Absolute block working.

is ON and to start braking immediately. Colour light signals' functions vary and we will cover those later. The layout will not have any distant signals – there is not enough space to warrant them but there could be if further baseboards were inserted between the station and fiddle yard boards. This has already been accommodated for with the wiring arrangements.

Double tracks are always described as 'up' and 'down' and the convention has been that trains always travel up to London, but there are local variations. At Scropton Crossing, up is towards Derby.

Under consideration is a train passing on the up line from signal box A to signal box B. There are terms to describe the relative positions of these boxes. The view taken is that of a train driver going along the line.

After passing box A, this signal box is said to be 'in the rear of' and signal box B would be 'in advance of' the train until the train passes it.

The table outlines the communication between the two signal boxes to pass a class 1 express passenger train from box A to box B.

When signal box B selects Line Clear, the signaller at box A can clear A's section signals to allow the train to enter section A. Otherwise a train might over-run into B where there might be an obstruction. Similarly, B cannot clear section B's signals until Line Clear has been received from the next up signal box.

Signal box A sends 2 bells when the train has passed Starter A.

An animated video with sound of absolute block working was produced by John Earwicker and uploaded to YouTube. This has the benefit of seeing what is happening to the signals in response to the various block movements (https://www.youtube.com/watch?v=eT_AVJjnotc). For 'signalman' in the video perhaps we can substitute signaller, as there are many women in signal boxes all over the country.

Now this may seem like a lot of bells for our layout just to get one train out of the fiddle yard and into the station. So, whilst absolute block is of historical (or possibly hysterical, if you are the one ringing the bells) significance, it would not suit the layout – we must find a simpler, yet still railway-like way, of operating the trains that will suit the layout's operation.

An outline of the communication between the two signal boxes, A and B, to pass a class 1 express passenger train between them

	Signal Box A			Signal Box B	
Bell	Meaning	Instrument	Bell	Meaning	Instrument
1	**Call Attention**	Normal	1	Attending	Normal
4	**Line Clear Express ?**	Normal	4	Line is clear for Express	Line Clear **selected**
	Reflects on UP line Dial	Line Clear			Line Clear
2	**Train entering section**	Line Clear	2	Acknowledge train entering section	Train on Line **selected**
	Reflects on UP line Dial	Train on line Train on line	2.1	**Train out of section**	Train on Line Train on Line
2.1	Acknowledge train out of section	Train on line			Normal **selected**
	Reflects on UP line Dial	Normal			Normal

The type in bold face indicates who instigates a communication and there is always a reply from the other box.

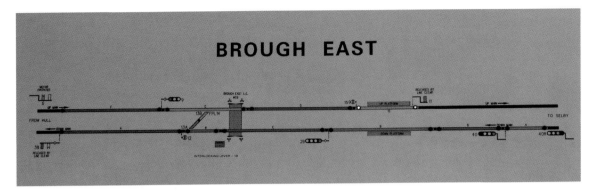

Fig. 127   Brough East signal box diagram.

TRACK CIRCUIT BLOCK (TCB)

Track circuit block is what most of the railway network now operates and is semi-automatic in some cases. Although this will not apply to the layout, we will have to operate any signals.

Originally, track circuits lit a lamp in a signal box to indicate where a train was. Then they were used to interlock block instruments, signals and points together to provide a safe working, absolute block signal environment.

Figure 127 is the diagram of Brough East signal box, which is on the Selby to Hull line in east Yorkshire. The two lights illuminated on the up line towards Selby are to indicate that a train is standing at the platform and this is a track circuit in operation, although we are in an absolute block area here. The track circuit is interlocked with the absolute block instruments, such that the signaller cannot select Line Clear on the block instrument, whilst the track circuit knows there is a train already present in the section. Note that the line is signalled with a mixture of semaphore and colour light signals. The next stage in the development of the track circuit was to actually have the track circuits controlling the signals, rather than just provide an indication.

With colour light signals it is possible to provide automatically changing signals that are controlled by the passage of trains or presence of vehicles on

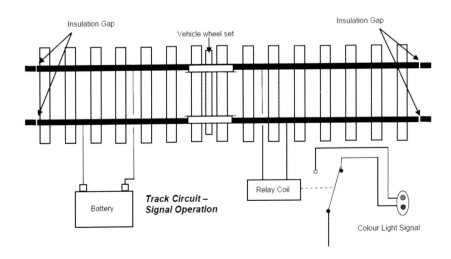

Fig. 128   Track circuit signal operation.

the track, but that is only possible on double-track running lines, which do not apply to our single-track lines.

The simplified diagram in Fig. 128 illustrates the principle. The track circuit consists of a power source that is connected to a circuit that is always broken unless a train's wheels are standing on the section of track guarded by the circuit. When a vehicle is present, it can energize the relay coil and change the aspect of the signal. If the power supply were to fail or the relay fail to operate, the system is fail-safe, like other railway equipment, and sets signals to ON or danger.

The reality is more complicated in the sense that colour light signals can display up to four aspects (or more if flashing colour lights are included). These additional aspects have been employed on track with high line-speeds and do not apply to our model but are included for interest. With continuous welded rail (CWR) the system has been changed from a simple DC circuit to one where AC is used and differing frequencies of voltage are employed to determine which section is which. A voltage of a certain frequency detected would indicate a train in a particular section that has that frequency. It is a bit like saying that if it is 88.1MHz frequency on the FM radio dial, it must be Radio 2.

The indications of a multiple aspect signal can be:

- Red – must not be passed at all.
- Double yellow – can be passed but expect caution at next signal; a kind of pre-warning.
- Yellow – caution, expect next signal to be at danger but can still be passed.
- Green – proceed.

TCB is primarily used where double up-and-down lines are employed, but can be used on some single lines. In the event of a train coming to a halt unexpectedly in a section, it is the guard or conductor's responsibility to protect the rear of the train by placing a shorting clip in the section beyond the one in which the train is standing. In TCB territory this would place preceding signals to danger. Network Rail term the clip a track circuit operating device

(TCOD). The guard is also obliged to put down explosive detonators on the track at a considerable distance from an unexpectedly halted train, which act as an audible alarm to a following train and the message is: 'apply emergency brakes'.

SINGLE-LINE WORKING

Single lines around Buxton use a key token, where the train driver has been issued with a physical token for that section of line. The token is usually housed in a machine in the signal box and the action of removing a token from the machine locks the token machine at the other end of the line, so that a train cannot be sent down in the opposite direction to that already occupied. It also locks signals in the reverse direction to danger or ON.

It is the driver's responsibility to check that the token for the correct line being travelled has been issued. It is the signaller's responsibility to ensure that the driver is issued with the token for that section of line being travelled. All this token-swapping considerably slows down the passage of trains and on our busy lines would not be appropriate and almost impossible to model with any degree of realism.

DOVEDALE WAY OF WORKING

The way in which a railway-like operation can be used to effect and still maintain interest and keep trains running is to use an abbreviated form of absolute block working where the station signal box is interfacing to a TCB area or, in our case, two TCB areas. What happens there is that trains are described using a block bell but that is all. As there is TCB, there is no need to give train entering section or train out of section bell codes with every train. TCB areas often provide axle counters to negate the need for train out of section and the track circuit knows when a train is in the section, so train entering section is not needed either.

An axle counter counts the numbers of axles entering a block section and compares this with the number of axles leaving the block section. If the two numbers are the same, the train can proceed as

Fig. 129   Gilberdyke Junction block bell train describer.

normal. If the two numbers differ, it usually means the train has become divided in the section and left vehicles behind on the track. In the latter case, the signals preceding the section can be set to ON or danger.

Figure 129 is a case in point on the prototype railway at Gilberdyke Junction on the Hull to Selby line. It is a picture of a block bell that is used to describe trains to Selby signal box, which is in a TCB area, and Selby rings the bell at Gilberdyke when it has a train to send. The morse tapper-type key is visible and one push on that rings the bell once at Selby and similarly the reverse is true at Gilberdyke.

On our layout we need a selectable indicator to tell the other signal box, be it station or fiddle yard, whether we are talking about the Chinley Junction line or the Buxton line. In reality there would be additional block bells for each line served but space in our situation is a factor and an indicator LED would be easily understood by both operators.

TRAIN CLASSIFICATION

There are ten different classifications of trains on

Classifications of trains on Network Rail

Classification Number	Meaning	Bell Code – number of beats
Class 1.	Express passenger train, postal or parcel or breakdown train proceeding to accident or snowplough.	4
Class 2.	Ordinary passenger train, breakdown train not proceeding to accident.	3 Pause 1
Class 3.	Freight train authorized to run at more than 75mph (120.7km/h) or specially authorized parcels or empty stock or NR Infrastructure train.	1 Pause 3 Pause 1
Class 4.	Freight train that can run up to 75mph (120.7km/h).	3 Pause 1 Pause 1
Class 5.	Empty stock passenger train.	2 Pause 2 Pause 1
Class 6.	Freight train that can run up to 60mph (96.6km/h).	5
Class 7.	Freight train that can run up to 45mph (72.4km/h).	4 Pause 1
Class 8.	Freight train that can run up to 35mph (56.3km/h) or less.	3 Pause 2
Class 9.	Class 373 Eurostar train.	1 pause 4
Class 0.	Light locomotive or locomotives coupled together.	2 pause 3

Network Rail, as given in the table, together with their train describer bell codes. In addition to bell codes, Network Rail uses a computer system called Trust that gives advance information of traffic movements and their running schedule to signallers.

We will not need Class 9 unless they route HS2 via Dovedale and several other classes can also be ruled out, which will leave us with:

- Class 1 the excursion DMU.
- Class 2 for normal DMU passenger working.
- Class 5 for the empty stock DMU returning to service to Chinley Junction and beyond, and its return later in the day to pick up excursionists.
- Class 6 for the usual limestone trains.
- Class 7 for returning empties.
- Class 0 for light engine movements.

There could be one more if it is decided to run Lafarge cement bogie hoppers through Dovedale, but for the moment these will suffice.

These trains and their bell codes will form the basis of operations at Dovedale and the foundation on which the sequence of operations will be written.

SIGNALLING

It was decided to use both semaphore and colour light signals, as that gives variety and is what is there now in the Buxton area in 2015.

The section on Absolute Block introduced the idea of home and distant signals, but as distances are short between signals on the layout, as they sometimes are in real life, then distant signals have been dispensed with; in real life there would be fixed distant signals giving a permanent caution to trains. Perhaps if more baseboards are inserted between the station and fiddle yard boards in the future, then the subject would come under review.

The semaphore signals under consideration are those to be found on the former London Midland Region of British Rail that originally belonged to the London Midland and Scottish Railway or LMSR. They are all of the upper-quadrant type in that the signal is raised above the horizontal to OFF or clear.

Fig. 130 Blackpool North Station platform starter signals.

Figure 130 shows the array of platform starter signals at Blackpool North Station and each of the bracket signals has two arms: one arm for each platform departure. The signal on the right is the seventh and last platform and so cannot be paired up with any other. Although it is usual to place signals to the left of the track it commands, as with ordinary traffic lights on the roads, here convenience and cost have intervened. Dovedale will have just such a platform starter bracket signal but will also need a further bracket signal, after the starters, to indicate to a train which branch it is taking. The complicated grey lattice system of hoops and extra railings will not be modelled, as that complicates matters no end and there are lots of unmodified signals on Network Rail as it is; the signal on the far right is a case in point.

Signal placement is all important as far as the view of them by the driver is concerned. Where there is any doubt as to which signal is for which track, an arrow plate attached to the signal post pointing to the track it refers to is employed.

Figure 131 shows the signalling around the freight-carrying lines around Great Rocks Junction

and the cement works at Tunstead. We saw a class 66 leaving the Lafarge works in Fig. 123.

The signal arms are now referred to as 'subsidiary', as they are never used to signal the movement of a passenger train. Not only that, the signals are not bracketed but subject to a process described by Network Rail as 'stacking'. These signals refer to a single line of track that has two different destinations and is completely at odds with the passenger line situation where we have two tracks referred to by one signal post, albeit bracketed with two arms. The stacking arm arrangement is only used on low-speed freight lines.

The stacking means that the single track is approaching a junction and the upper signal refers to a track on the left and the lower signal refers to track on the right. If there had been another signal on the post below the two already on the post, then that would refer to a track to the right of the middle one.

So, in practice the line leaves the Tunstead cement works and splits into two. The left-hand line is the goods' loop, where a train can be held for a time, and the right-hand line is the running line to Peak

Fig. 131 Great Rocks Junction subsidiary signals.

Fig. 132 Great Rocks Junction subsidiary signals pulled off for a departure.

Forest, Chinley Junction and beyond. The class 66 and cement train are clearly taking the right-hand line from the semaphore signal that is off (Fig. 123).

The same class 66 and train are heading towards Peak Forest South on their way to Chinley Junction (Fig. 124). You can just see the goods' loop previously referred to on the left of the train. The running line signals are giving a cautious go to the train but the distant signal remains ON. As Peak Forest South signal box is just by the class 60, this is quite normal practice.

We will need two stacking subsidiary arms signals at Dovedale. Both are needed to exit the freight reception roads.

Back to Fig. 131 and a detail on the signal post is the plate with the GSM-R telephone number of 7471 6101. GSM-R is the Global System for Mobile Communications, as used by European railways. The technology is the same as used by mobile 'phone companies but it is a private network. Earlier organizational systems used the commercial mobile phone networks but they found that the system would freeze on New Year's Eve, as everyone was sending SMS greetings and coverage was no use in cuttings and tunnels. Coverage is guaranteed on Network Rail, as it has its own aerials trackside, many of which are placed by signal boxes.

The purpose of placing the number on the posts

is to enable a driver whose train is held at the signal to enquire of the signal box when progress is likely. This is Rule 55 and used to be enabled by the use of telephones attached to the posts; this is still to be found on Network Rail in places.

The telephone number is the same for each signal that is controlled by the same signal box. So, 7471 6101 is Great Rocks Junction signal box's telephone number. The GSM-R system has many others uses and if you type 'gsm-r handbook' into your browser, that will produce a PDF document on the subject. (You will need Adobe reader installed on your device before you can open the file.)

Now for more detail, with Fig. 124. On the signal post of the home and distant bracket signal facing us is a lozenge, hexagonal-shaped white plate. This is to indicate to train drivers that the track is track circuited and that, in consequence, there is no need to call the signaller if stopped at the signal, as the signaller is aware of the train's presence in the same way that we saw in the example at Brough East in Fig. 127.

Figure 132 is a view looking back down the track at Tunstead Works and there is a further signal arm OFF to enable the class 66 and train to leave Lafarge's premises and end up on Network Rail tracks. Note the grey Lafarge shunter lurking on the works' tracks. The two signals on the same post

Fig. 133   Fiddler's Ferry Power Station, and class 70 arrives with loaded coal train.

by the 15mph (25km/h) sign perform the same function as we saw for Fig. 123, but for the single-track
branch to Buxton, which is on the extreme left
of Fig. 132. The lifting barber's pole barrier is the
demarcation point between Lafarge and Network
Rail, although Network Rail's Great Rocks Junction
signal box controls all the signals.

Another load of imported coal is on its way to
Fiddler's Ferry Power Station with Freightliner class
70, 70 006 in charge of the coal hopper wagons (Fig.
133). Note that the subsidiary arm is signalling the
train over the crossover in the foreground and into
the power station loops from the main line. The
circular gadget right by the smaller arm is a position
transmitter, which relays the signal's status back to
the signal box. Handy if the signal is out of sight of
the signal box but slightly mystifying here, as the box
is right behind the camera.

Fig. 134   Fiddler's Ferry Power Station, and class 60 departs with empties.

Note the signal wires on steel posts running either side of the tracks and the ground disc signal with its back to us on the left.

The 15mph (25km/h) speed limit on the period sign refers to the crossover into the power station. Note also that the points here are electrically operated, and one of the grey motor housings is by the speed restriction sign, even though the crossover is right by the box.

Figure 134 is again at Fiddler's Ferry near Warrington, only this time a DB Schenker class 60, 60 044 is leaving the unloading loops with EWS branded empties at the power station. The signals have been modernized and are no longer subsidiary arms. They are the same size as the main line running signal on the far left. Plenty of signal wires here and at least one of them is taut.

Noteworthy is that the coal supply contract is shared between Freightliner and DB Schenker, introducing more variety for stock haulage.

Figure 135 sees a return to Peak Forest South and the location is at the top of the gradient shown in Fig. 124, with the departing Lafarge train we saw, looking back towards Great Rocks Junction. The class 60 in Fig. 124 is behind the signal box on the right. The double-track running lines are in the centre of the picture flanked by two goods' loops. The class 66 shunting the crushed limestone train on the left is occupying one of them and has just moved the train out of the Cemex track area. The home and distant signals on the post and further down on the bracket are for the main running line on the left of the pair in the centre of the picture, and so remain at danger.

The goods' loop on the right-hand side has a subsidiary armed exit signal on the same bracket as the main running line home signal.

There are plenty of ground signals about and they are mainly for reversing moves. A basic principle is that no train should move unless there is a signal to

Fig. 135   Peak Forest South, and class 66 shunts limestone train.

Fig. 136 Fiddler's Ferry Power Station, and class 66 reverses past ground signal.

authorize it. The ground disc at the bottom of the picture is for a move from the right-hand running line, where trains would normally run towards the camera, reversing over the crossover. Note that not all possible moves are signalled, and these moves, if attempted, would be termed illegal. If it were opera-tionally essential that a so-called illegal move was needed, it would be executed by the use of hand signals from the signaller using either a three-col-oured Bardic lamp or flags. Note the stacked ground disc with its back to us; they use the same method of operation as the stacked subsidiary armed signals

Fig. 137 Gaerwen track layout and signals.

we saw. Ground discs can also be used as siding exit signals but not for passenger trains with passengers in them.

The ground discs all have a white-painted arm at the rear and a rearward facing light, so that the signaller can tell that the signal has answered the lever, if the rear of the signal is facing the box.

The model may incorporate some ground signals but getting them to work in 4mm is tricky, unless you've spent at least ten years working for Rolex or some other Swiss timepiece manufacturer.

Figure 136 sees a return to near Warrington at Fiddler's Ferry Power Station signal box. The class 66 has moved up the main line on the right out of the run-round loops. It has come to a stand and is now signalled for a reversing move back into a different siding to pick up fly ash hoppers. Note that the ground disc is signalling the move but with the addition of an illuminated 'stencil box' that gives the siding ident. Where the locomotive is going is siding C. Note the GSM-R plate and number for Fiddler's Ferry signal box.

Figure 137 is at Gaerwen on Anglesey (Ynys Môn)

and shows us another ground disc for reversing over the crossover. In addition, though, there is a clue as to how the signalling works. The grey box contains a device known as a detection slide and this is connected to the point tie-bar. It works in a similar way to the facing point lock mechanism we saw in Fig. 33, but this time it is an interlock such that the ground signal cannot be pulled off unless the point is in the correct position. Note also the surviving ground disc to signal a reversing move onto the now severed Amlwch branch line.

The point rods that go to the signal box and the signal wires that go there too are also interlocked in a mechanical frame, which is usually underneath the lever frame where the signaller is. Some points and signals have electrical solenoid locking, if it is not convenient to incorporate it mechanically.

Figure 138 shows the cut-down lever frame at Scropton Crossing on the Stoke-on-Trent to Derby line. A yellow lever is a distant signal, a red lever a home signal and a black lever number 13 is for points. In this case it is a crossover and one lever operates both points, as they are mechanically linked. The

Fig. 138 Scropton signal box lever frame.

white levers are disused functions. The locking lever frame is downstairs but of interest here is lever 3, and the significance here is that it is also electrically locked, as well as mechanically. The white stripe signifies that and we can see a black box on the floor by the lever that has wires coming out of it, which is the connection to a solenoid that locks other functions, probably to do with the crossing gates. We can also see from the labelling on lever 1, the distant signal, that levers 2 and 3 must be pulled before number 1. This is part of the mechanical locking in the frame and means that the signaller cannot set the distant signal to OFF or clear unless the home signals were also OFF.

Colour light signals are interlocked either by relays or by a solid state circuit. A solid state circuit uses semiconductors and micro-processors or computer chips that allow the interlocking to be programmable and can introduce such features as time-delays together with a networking feature, such that large areas can be interlocked, which would not be possible with a mechanical system – even with solenoid interlocking.

Interlocking will be included in the model by relays for both semaphore and colour light signals.

ASPECTS OF SIGNALLING IN THE MODEL OF DOVEDALE

SIGNAL INTERLOCKING

Figure 139 is a diagram of the principle of interlocking the points and signals at Dovedale. The circuit to the signal motor is interrupted by the placement of a relay contact, which is normally closed or is made

when the power is off to the relay coil. This relay contact is operated and the contacts opened when any one of the point motor supplies is energized. We have seen that the point motor supplies are energized in both directions and the trick is to choose the one that will conflict with our signal selection. For example, with the platform bracket signal, if the point that gives access to the platform and signal we are concerned with is set against access to that platform, then it is the positive supply that makes the point move to that position we are interested in.

However, this is not rocket science because if the choice is incorrect, we simply swap it over to the other choice on the point motor. We are looking for the relay to operate when any point in the path of a signal is set against it, thereby locking the signal out.

The big difference between this interlocking and Network Rail is that on the model, if the signal is selected to OFF or go and we then move a point motor switch in its path, the signal will return to danger automatically as the lockout relay will still operate. On Network Rail, the signal would lock out any further point movement.

There are those who advocate that the track power could be applied if the correct route with the signals was set, but that is un-prototypical and in any case would introduce problems with bi-directional working. In other words, if you wanted to reverse a train, the signals for the opposite direction would have to be pulled, which is nonsense.

Train drivers have always had the option to pass a signal at danger and so it remains here, although use of the signals will avoid such embarrassing moments as the passenger train setting off for Buxton only

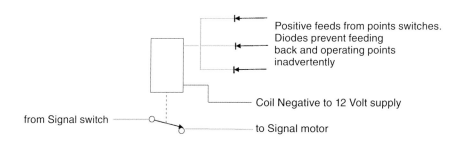

Fig. 139 Point and signal interlocking.

to derail on the double-slip because it wasn't set correctly.

The introduction of the European Rail Traffic Management System (ERTMS) throughout the network will do away with lineside signals and a computer on the train will be making many of the crucial decisions. The case for its introduction is made all the stronger because recent incidents in the USA and Spain, causing loss of life, were due to train drivers speeding.

SECTION INTERLOCKING

The way of moving trains at Dovedale requires that the station operator drives trains both out of and into the fiddle yard. The fiddle yard operator has to ensure that a train, on arrival, is correctly set onto a vacant traverser road or part road if it's a DMU and switch the train off when it has arrived. This means that the station controller power must be switchable by the fiddle yard operator so that the station controller can drive trains in and out of the fiddle yard. Trains coming into the fiddle yard will pass colour light signals under the control of the fiddle yard operator and they must be interlocked with the nearest double-slip motor to the fiddle yard.

In addition, the track power for the station controller selected into the fiddle yard must be interlocked with the signals too. If they weren't, it could mean that a train setting off from Dovedale Station could reach one of the fiddle yard colour light signals at green and then stop if the controller switchover had not been selected for Dovedale Station.

This is an easy mistake to make but demeans the operating ethos. With the system as modelled, the colour light signal could not be pulled off until the correct selection for station track power had been made. As all trains are under the direct visual supervision of operators there is no

requirement for track circuits, although in Chapter 7 we shall investigate what can be done to supervise trains properly when they are not under direct visual control.

There are signals for the entry to Dovedale Station but these are 'off stage' or beyond the fiddle yard tunnel-mouth. If further baseboards were inserted between the station and fiddle yard, these signals would need to be modelled; extra cabling has

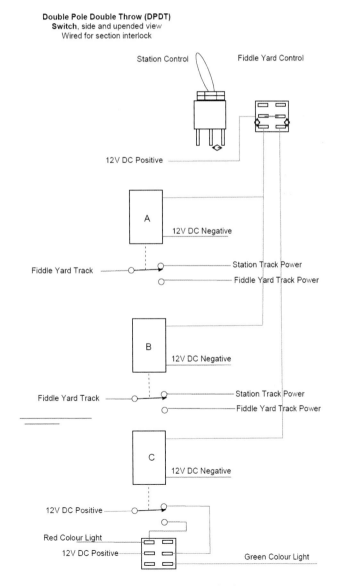

Fig. 140 Fiddle yard section switch interlocking.

been wired into the connectors at the initial building stage to accommodate just such an update.

Figure 140 shows the circuit diagram that is needed to be built to ensure the section interlock previously mentioned in the last but one paragraph.

First of all some explanation is needed as to colour coding the track power cables. Right from the off it was decided to adopt the convention that, looking towards the buffer stops at Dovedale, the left-hand track would use a red wire for track power and the right-hand track would use black. This just makes life easier when wiring point frogs and section switches. It is not a polarity thing, as we know that polarity swaps around when the locomotive is reversed.

The section changeover switch at the top of Fig. 140 operates to supply two relays, A and B, with DC to change them over. In the diagram, the station controller has been selected by the fiddle yard operator and so both relays are energized and station controller power is selected to the fiddle yard tracks. The other side of the top DPDT switch supplies a further 12V DC to yet another relay, C. This is necessary as with colour lights we need to have some power fed to some signal all the time. You may recall that with semaphore signals, in the ON or danger position, there is no power applied and so life is simpler. What this means is that we must supply the red colour light signal, even if the green is selected but locked out because the fiddle yard operator has not selected the station controller track feed.

In Fig. 140 we have station controller selected and so the way is clear, if we have the green colour light selected, for that aspect to be energized. If we have selected green on the signal but not the station controller track feed, then relay C will be de-energized and no green aspect can be displayed but the red signal will still be fed with power from the normally closed contact on relay C.

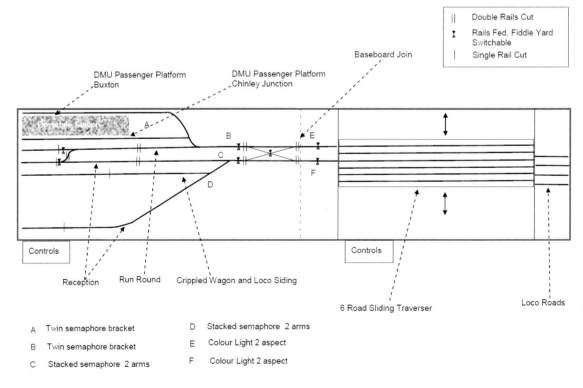

A   Twin semaphore bracket   D   Stacked semaphore 2 arms
B   Twin semaphore bracket   E   Colour Light 2 aspect
C   Stacked semaphore 2 arms   F   Colour Light 2 aspect

Fig. 141   Final Dovedale layout plan.

Without relay C, if we had selected green on the colour light switch but had not selected station controller track power, there would have been no aspect on the colour light signal at all, which is not as it is in real life with the fail-safe system on Network Rail.

There need to be two such circuits: one for each approach track at the fiddle yard. So it is perfectly possible for one road to be station controller selected, whilst the other is fiddle yard controller selected, although both tracks do not actually line up together with the traverser, which is intentional.

LAYOUT SIGNALLING AND FINAL TRACK PLAN

Figure 141 is the final, as-built track plan and it has been updated to include signals and their positions.

Operating rationale: the fiddle yard is as proposed and must be capable of handling:

- 2 × 2-car DMUs.
- 1 × single-car DMU.
- 3 × 3-car freight trains and locos.

The normal 3-car freight trains arrive from Chinley and depart to Buxton, running round on the crossover. The 3-car empties can optionally go on the back reception road nearest the controller. This will require a further loco to take the train out whilst the original loco waits for the next train of empties or as a standby for the full trains. A loco needs to be positioned at the start of the sequence, of which more later, in the loco/crippled siding.

Passenger trains occupy a simplified and cut-down version of the original station and the remnant of one of the original platforms is modelled together with some track that betrays the original spacious four-platform layout. The service platforms have been cut back to accommodate 2-car DMUs and are devoid of ramps and locomotive run-round facilities as a consequence. Figure 142 is an example of abandoned platforms and track at Crewe Station in contrast to a platform where the track has simply been removed, as we saw in Fig. 121.

The two bracket signals, because they signal passenger trains, must have regular-sized 4ft arms (1.2m) but the freight stacked signals can be either 3ft or 4ft, as we saw at Great Rocks Junction and Fiddler's Ferry. The two colour light signals are simple twin aspect red/green signals and interlocked with not only the double-slip, but the fiddle yard and station controllers There are no incoming signals for trains arriving at the station, there isn't room, but this would be modelled if and when extra boards were inserted.

There will be some use of un-coupler ramps, as we saw during the fiddle yard construction.

Fig. 142   Crewe Station abandoned platforms.

CHAPTER FIVE

ELEMENTS OF INTEGRATION

INTRODUCTION

This chapter is not intended to be a blow-by-blow account of how the layout was built, as by its nature some aspects of it are repetitive and once you have installed one set of track droppers, you have the T shirt in that department. We have already seen the principles and building blocks that will go to make up the layout and now it is time to get it all to work effectively and reliably.

The order of the text is the order that the actual construction took place, so some areas covered in the workshop phase are returned to, when appropriate, in this phase. Projects of this kind are like that and it is seldom possible to draw a line under some section early on and describe it as finished.

TRACK DROPPERS

This unlikely term is a reference to the use of a piece of brass wire to convey track supply to the actual rails. They are important in the sense that they must be unobtrusive and a piece of multi-cored cable soldered to the rails would not be.

Centre stage of Fig. 143 is a track dropper installed but as yet unpainted with rail colour. The 24 AWG wire is the same we used on the sliding cupboard traverser deck-locking mechanism in Fig. 66. It needs to be about 3in (75mm) long with a ²⁄₅in (10mm) right-angled cranked piece at one end, which is dipped in the flux first and then tinned before we offer it to the rail. The rail has to be scraped clean of the rail colour paint we applied and then fluxed and tinned. Apply the iron to the fluxed area until the solder flows into the rail web. Drill a ¹⁄₁₆in (1.5mm) hole as close to the rail as you can and feed the dropper in.

The right-angled cranked ²⁄₅in (10mm) piece now makes sense as it is that bit that stops it falling through the hole to the floor beneath. Gather up the dropper and hold it against the rail and apply the soldering iron to the rail and dropper together. It can make it easier to use a small clip called a miniature crocodile clip (eBay £1.80 for ten) to hold the dropper wire against the rail. Beware

Fig. 143 Point and track gaps and connection detail.

of holding the iron on there too long or you will have a crocodile clip soldered to the track, which is not recommended. As soon as the solder starts to melt, remove the iron and all will be well. The crocodile clip acts as a heat 'sink' or shunt and will conduct excess heat away, which will make it more difficult to solder the clip to the track anyway. Also, keeping the conduction of heat down minimizes the number of melted sleepers, but to achieve this, the iron must be hot so that the solder is melted quickly and the joint formed.

This heat conduction is a useful property that is often used when soldering LEDs and other delicate electronic products. The clip attached to a connecting leg will stop an LED from being melted.

Note the brass pins lightly holding the track down; these will be removed or hammered in after ballasting, and painted over with matt black as per track colour.

Also in view on the inside of one of the rails, towards the top of the picture, a panel pin has been hammered in to maintain the gauge if the sleepers don't feel like doing it any more. Either the panel pin will just sit there if the rail's tendency is to bear against it or the panel pin will need to be soldered to the rail to keep it in position. Make sure, if the panel pin is on the inside of a rail, that it is hammered in far enough to impinge on the bottom web of the rail, as shown; this will avoid any wheel flange hitting it.

Figure 144 shows the underside of the station board at the buffer-stop end and a view of the south end of a track dropper. The protruding wire is twisted around on itself to make a loop and then fluxed and tinned. We know from the wire colour convention established in the last chapter that the red rail is the left-hand rail and black the right-hand, looking towards the buffer stops.

Note that there is a 1in (25mm) hole drilled in the baseboard cross-timber to accommodate all the wiring and the three eight-way cables labelled A, B and C are already in position. Here they are shown wired in parallel with another track feed, but before we connect the second set of wires we need to test this bit first. Cut red and black wires, 6½ft (2m) long, and terminate them in the miniature crocodile

Fig. 144   Below-baseboard dropper connections.

clips, of the type we've just used as a heat sink, and connect these to the 12V controller. Connect the crocodile clips to the droppers and make sure a loco runs okay on the bit that the droppers are attached to. If there is a short-circuit, make sure that is fixed before we go onto the next pair of droppers.

It takes longer to describe it than to do it and may save time later when a short-circuit appears and we don't know where it might be as all droppers are now paralleled up. There aren't any point frogs wired up yet so journeys will be short, but at least we will know what the fault is not, if one appears.

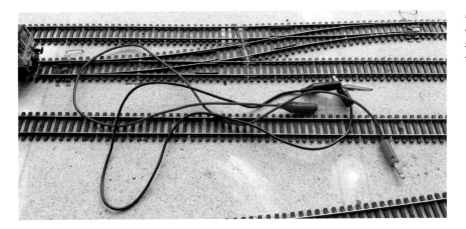

Fig. 145   Crossover configuration and supplied power supply test leads.

Figure 145 shows the test cable supplied with the power supplies from Circuit Specialists and, although a little short, it can be adapted to be our track supply test cable. The 4mm plugs are particularly useful, as they just plug in and out to and from the power supply.

POINT MOTOR INSTALLATION – MECHANICAL

Going back to Fig. 103 (Chapter 3 'Point Motors'), we made up eight kits of point motor together with their associated frog changeover relays and the point motor was motored to the approximate mid-position as it says on the tin or Fulgurex instructions. We just use the test cable, as in Fig. 145, with the controller set to 12V. Remove the power when you get to the mid-position.

Fig. 146   Fulgurex point motor actuating lever – first fitting.

Figure 96 (Chapter 3 'Point Motors') showed us the Fulgurex-supplied point motor actuating lever and tube that will convey point motor movement below baseboard level to point tie-bar above it. This also absolves us of the tedious process of hewing large chunks out of the baseboard to accommodate the point change-over mechanism.

With reference to Fig. 146:

1. Form a loop on the point tie-bar brass wire about ⅖in (10mm) from the end of the tie-bar. The actual distance will depend on whether there are any adjacent tracks.
2. Using the Fulgurex actuating arm and tube as a guide, mark off with the felt-tipped pen on the baseboard a 1⁄16in (1.5mm) drill hole position.
3. Drill the hole vertically and lightly tap the tube and arm into position, as shown in the Fig. 147. Use a piece of scrap wood as a buffer and the smallest hammer, or even push using your fingers. Engage the arm on the tie-bar and crimp the loop on the tie-bar with a pair of snipe-nose pliers. Figure 147 shows us the finished item.
4. Now go under the board and mark off on the tube a point that leaves the tube about ⅕in (5mm) clear from the underside of the board. In other words, we need the tube to protrude a bit to provide a bearing for the arm to operate. There should be no issues with baseboard cross-struts getting in the way, as we have designed this out.

*Fig. 147 Fulgurex point motor actuating lever –
second fitting.*

*Fig. 148 Fulgurex point motor actuating lever –
third fitting.*

5. Cut the tube in the tube-cutter to that value
   and refit. The actual length of the complete
   tube in this case is ¾in (20mm), ½in (12mm) for
   the baseboard and two bits either side to act as
   bearing surfaces and to stop the actuating arm
   moving vertically. You will have to ream or file
   out the tube after cutting to restore the tube
   internal diameter. Keep any tube remnants.

Figure 148 shows the refitted tube and arm after
trimming the tube from the baseboard underside.
There is another one to its left and this is the double-slip. The two feeds to the centre of the device
are on the left and as they are fairly close to each
other at ⅔in (16.5mm) or thereabouts, they have
been fitted with heat-shrink sleeves to avoid short-
circuits.

The actuating arm is bent at right angles and in the
direction we want the point motor to go (Fig. 149).
In other words, the motor will fit either towards
the top or bottom of the picture, thereby avoiding
the feeds on the left or one of the double-slip frogs
on the right.

Make a loop that is big enough to contain the
1.2mm brass rod, which we have used on the tie-
bars previously; this is going to connect the motor
to the actuating arm. We can crimp the loop up
later after the motor has been fitted.

The Z actuating arm is now connected to the
point tie-bar, so we can position the unit to take the
point motor. First though, make sure the Z arm and
point tie-bar are free to move smoothly.

As the point motor has been motored to the
mid-position with our power supply/controller, the
point tie-bar needs to be in that same position. This
is easily done by clipping two crocodile clips, one
on each running rail on the point near the tie-bar
and between running and moving rails. These will
force the moving point blades to the mid-position
and keep them there.

Fit a piece of brass wire, about 2–3in (50–75mm)
long to the point motor on either end. The only
consideration is where the terminals are near any
other item underneath the board. The brass wire
must form a U-shape at one end but not so big a U
that it fouls the plastic moulding of the point base
when the sliding shaft retracts. The other end needs
a right angle of about ⅖in (10mm) bending in it.

Offer up the point motor and engage the right
angle in the loop, seen previously in Fig. 149, and
hold in position. Punch a hole in the screw hole

*Fig. 149 Fulgurex point motor actuating lever –
fourth fitting.*

Fig. 150   Fulgurex point motor actuating lever – final fitting.

nearest the brass wire arm using a sharp-pointed screwdriver or, alternatively, mark the screw hole spot with a felt-tipped pen, remove the motor and then punch a hole.

Screw the point motor in position with one screw first of all and be careful not to over-tighten. Now manoeuvre the point motor about the single screw until it best lines up with the actuating arm. Now mark and insert the other screw. If you use the no.8 woodscrew, as in the example, you may need to drill out the base of the point motor first to accept it.

Figure 150 shows the point motor fitted and a point to note (sorry!) is that if we undo two screws, the point motor is released by unhooking the arm from the loop. It is not fixed and doesn't need to be. The next step is to remove the crocodile clips from the running rails and to power up the motor with the pair of leads we made earlier; make sure the motor works by first applying one polarity and then the other. If the motor groans or complains, check that it is not too tightly screwed down and that the 1.2mm brass arm is not fouling the underside of the point motor base.

Any excess movement will be taken up with the springiness in the Z arm. If by some happenstance the point blades do not 'make' in both directions, you can tweak the movement by bending the Fulgurex rod above the baseboard, as it has been slightly in

Fig. 147. All of this will be painted rail colour and so will hardly be visible on the layout.

Two items worthy of note are:

- If the cranked arm below the baseboard is shorter than the arm above that moves the tie-bar, this will mean that there will be amplification of the movement but reduction in delivered force. Conversely, if the arm underneath is longer than the one on top, the total movement will be reduced but force amplified. This is simply how levers work. In the example, the lower arm is slightly longer than the upper, so the movement or throw is slightly amplified.
- If there is slop in the two loops at the tie-bar and below the baseboard, there will be what is known as 'lost motion'. This means that the point motor will move a bit but nothing else will until the slack is taken up. This can mean, if there is lots of lost motion, that the point will not change over correctly.

As usual in engineering it is a compromise between having a linkage that is free to move but not that free that the point motor doesn't do its job right.

The not-to-scale diagram in Fig. 151 summarizes what has been said about Z arms. Of note is that the legs of the connecting linkages do not have to be in the same plane as we can see from the lower drawing.

The connecting of the frog will have to wait until we have a control panel with switches in to operate the point motor.

CONTROL PANEL AND WIRING

In Chapter 3, we got to a stage where the stabilized power supply controller was fitted into the purpose-built control panel with its aluminium sheet panel. The controller was wired to a DPDT switch but that was all.

Now that items such as the point motors are physically in position and they work remotely using the made-up cable, the next step is to install a power supply for the point motors and connect it all up. Then the point motors will answer the call of a switch on the control panel and the frogs will change over so that trains can run.

Figure 152 shows the 12V DC power supply we wired up for mains' use in Chapter 3. The two mounting slots have been used to screw the supply to the edge of the control panel frame and these are the same type of screws used on the traverser deck locking mechanism, countersunk no.8 ½in (12mm). What is important here is that enough room is left to clear the switches that are mounted on the aluminium panel when that is fitted, about ⅗in (15mm) – though it depends on the switches you have.

The mains lead has been taken underneath the power supply and the lead has been strain-relieved by the white co-axial cable clip (eBay – 100 items for £1.79 delivered). This will reduce the possibility of tension on the mains cable, resulting in the mains cables being pulled out of the terminal block. Another wheeze is to fasten the mains cable to the clip using a cable tie, but more of cable ties later.

Before we plug the mains in though, the 12V DC is taken out using orange and blue cables for positive and negative, respectively, and secured to the edge of the panel with a piece of chocolate block. Into the chocolate block will be connected all the 12V DC fixed supply equipment: points, signals, lights and block bells. Note that the track power, red and black, goes off to the A cable on the controller to station board connector and we can immediately distinguish between track and fixed power supply cabling.

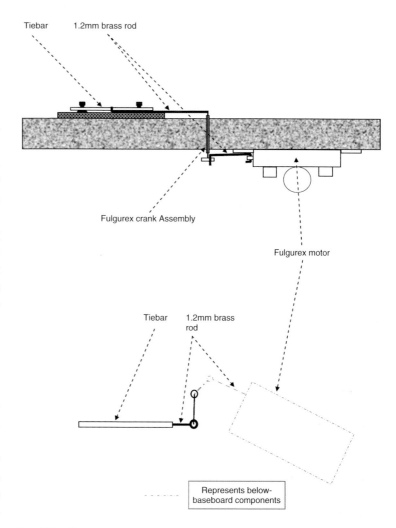

Fig. 151   Diagram of point motor mechanical installation.

Fig. 152   12V DC power supply wired up and in circuit.

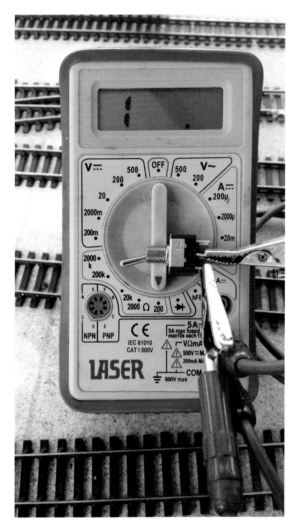

Fig. 153 DPDT switch under test and open circuit shown on meter.

The meter shows the amount of resistance in the circuit between the two contacts. The reading means the resistance is so large it can't be measured. This means the switch operates in the opposite way to that shown and is as described above. When the switch toggle is changed over, the reading would be 0.003 or 0.004, indicating a circuit. The circuit uses a small battery inside the meter and is perfectly safe and would not harm the equipment.

Now we have the way the switch works sorted, we can mount the switches so that a selection on a switch is indicated by the switch toggle position.

We have seven switches made up into kits ready to mount onto the panel (Fig. 154). The switches are wired as shown at the bottom of Fig. 113, except that the orange and blue cables are soldered to the centre pair of switch contacts; it does not matter which way round they go. There are eight point motors and only seven levers, as one pair of points is a crossover and only requires one switch to operate it. The wires are twisted together to maintain neatness when installed.

With mechanical levers in signal boxes, one lever operates two points on a crossover and the points have interconnected rodding to achieve this. On the diagram of Scropton Crossing at Fig. 125 (Chapter 4 'Absolute Block'), lever 13 operates the crossover and the points are described as 13A and 13B.

The orange and blue cables will go into the chocolate block we saw at Fig. 151 and this time it does matter which way round the cables go.

Figure 153 is a picture of the test of how the DPDT switch actually operates. Before we mount these switches we need to know this as the switch toggle position will tell us what will happen to the point motor if we change it. Figure 113 (Chapter 3 'Control Panel') shows how most switches work. When the toggle is in one position, the opposite set of contacts is connected to the middle pair. This is because the switch usually operates on a spring-loaded rocker. However, they are not all the same and so a means of finding this out is handy. We can also test items that are suspect.

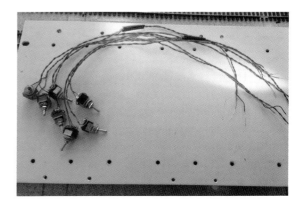

Fig. 154 Point motor switches made up in kit form.

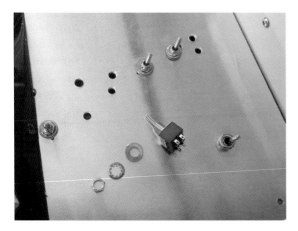

Fig. 155 Point motor switches in component form and fitted.

Figure 155 shows the DPDT switch in kit form with the black protective covering on the aluminium panel partially peeled back to reveal the panel surface.

The switches' mounting assembly consists of:

1. A locking washer, which engages with a channel on the threaded part of the switch barrel, and also a hole drilled in the panel to stop it all from turning.
2. A further spring locking washer.
3. A securing nut.
4. In addition, there is usually also a nut underneath the locking washer, which is used to vary the height above which the switch appears on a panel. We shall not need this extra nut and it should be removed and kept.

The three components are assembled in that order. The switches vary slightly as to the size of hole needed in the panel; the ones shown needed a 5.5mm drill but some need a 6mm drill or almost ¼in in Imperial units. Some of the sellers on eBay provide a drawing with the listing with the information on it; if not you'll have to measure it by using a ruler on the inside of one of the locking washers.

When the hole has been drilled you can offer up the switch to appear within the hole and then fit the locking washer loosely. The convention adopted here was that the switch position indicates the direction that the point blades would move to when operated. You can use LEDs on the panel to indicate that but that is a lot of extra work. However, we will use LEDs for the double-slip to indicate which tracks are selected. The only place where this doesn't work is the crossover, and the convention used there was up for straight lines and down for crossover. However, this is down to personal choice.

When you have the correct orientation of the switch, mark off the position where the locking tab on the locking washer will go with a felt-tipped pen on the panel. Drill a 1.5mm hole where the locking tab slots into. It does not matter much if this is slightly inaccurate, as we can bend the tab to suit later. It does not really matter if you drill the hole 90 degrees from where it is needed, as you can drill another hole in the right place and the original will hardly show under the locking and spring washers.

If we subsequently find that the motor operates in the opposite sense to that we require, then we simply swap the chocolate block connections at the motor, as we saw in Fig. 103 (Chapter 3).

Figure 155 shows some switches fitted with the locking tab in position. The nut is tightened with a pair of ordinary pliers held vertically so as not to scratch the aluminium surface. The essential thing is to tighten carefully so that the spring washer is just engaged. Too tight and you will separate the switch barrel from the switch body. If the switch body has rotated slightly, use your fingers to straighten it up from the underside. If you use a long-reach socket and ratchet handle, it is all the easier to break the switch in half.

Point motor switches can then be connected up to the 12V fixed supply chocolate block.

There is a warts-and-all view of the rear of the panel and some point motor switches in Fig. 156. The drilled holes have been tidied up of burrs with a 10mm drill held by hand and twisted. Ensure that any power supply fitted in the panel is protected from swarf and switched off when carrying out this work.

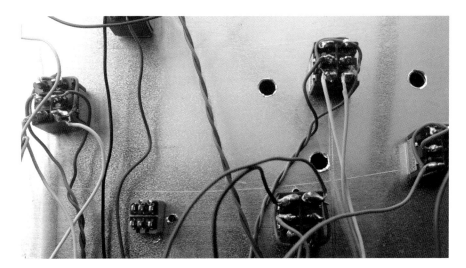

Fig. 156 Point motor switches, rear control panel view.

Before wiring up any point motors, just remove the DC fixed mains from the wall socket. The fixed power supply has short-circuit protection but it is still good practice to disconnect whilst working on the wiring.

The point motor switch near the bottom-right has the centre cables of orange and blue, as we made up in the kit, but now has the addition of the brown and green wires from cable group A added to connect to the motor. The switch above it and to the right has yellow and white cables from cable group A and the switch on the extreme left also has yellow and white but this time from cable group B. It

doesn't really matter to which pair of outside switch terminals these connections are wired to because, if the motor does not operate in the correct sense, we simply swap the DC supply at the motor end.

The smaller switch without any connections to it is a signal motor switch and we only need one pole of make/break for this. The same type was used for section switches.

The panel wiring has moved on a bit and we now have all seven point motor switches wired up (Fig. 157). The eighth DPDT switch at the top-right is the locomotive reversing switch, as we can see from the red and black cables. A red cable has been taken

Fig. 157 Rear control panel view with smaller section switches.

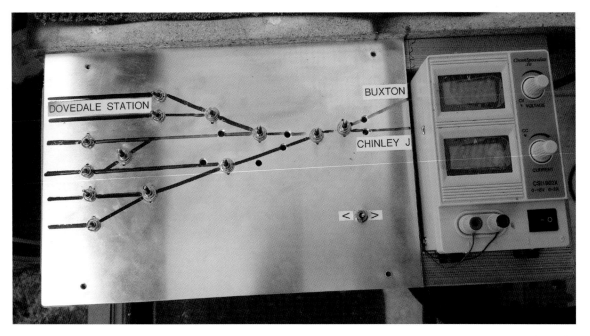

Fig. 158 Dovedale control panel with just two signal switches fitted.

from the chocolate block, bottom-right, around the panel to the four section switches that are located at the ends of sidings. The passenger DMU platforms do not have section switches. We only need one cable to potentially supply all sections.

We also know that the siding droppers are all the rails nearest the operator from our convention, or alternatively, if we cut the rails nearest the operator, it must be supplied from the red side. The section switches are the four smaller switches on the left-hand side.

The two smaller switches yet to be wired are for the bracket signal at Dovedale Station platforms.

Those who have no need to go to Specsavers will have spotted that the white and yellow cables make a further appearance on the section switches, this time cable group C.

Figure 158 shows the flip or operator's side of the panel with the switch positions joined up with the black felt-tipped pen to give a track diagram; this will need tidying up when the installation is complete. This configuration has the convenience of being able to see which switch operates what,

whereas with a traditional signal box diagram you have to be able to relate numbers on the diagram to numbers on the levers. This kind of layout is popular with small, modernized installations in signal boxes. The modern Railway Operating Centres that will replace all other signal boxes use VDUs and tracker balls, or mouse-like devices, to operate functions.

The VDUs are functionally connected by software to produce a continuous linear display, where each VDU represents a length of track or tracks. Clickable functions are interlocked by Solid State Interlocking, which is controlled by a microprocessor that supervises programmable logic functions. This means it is very easy to change the interlocking should the functional railway require it.

Note that the switches for points and signals are coloured black and red, respectively, as they are in a real signal box, and the section switches are uncoloured. Light switches when fitted will be similarly uncoloured but labelled.

The panel at this stage is a work in progress and, in addition to the signal switches, indicator LEDs will be fitted.

Beneath the control panel will be fitted the inter-locking logic controller that will be fabricated from relays and diodes, as described in Chapter 4 'Signal Interlocking' (Fig. 139). We need a lockout relay for each signal and a diode for each point that is concerned in the interlocking. However, if a point is used in the interlocking of say, three signals, we only need one diode and one feed.

The fiddle yard controller controls the two signals at the tunnel mouth into the fiddle yard and that will have its own relay panel but will need inputs through the wiring from the double-slip point motor at the far end of the station board. In other words, the actual junction to the two branch lines' part of the track layout. The inner double-slip point motor interlocking is all to do with the station area signals.

We have seen the relatively simple way in which the point motor switches are wired with just two coloured cables coming from the switch to the cable group A or B or C.

At the point motor end, we need to refer back to Chapter 3 'Point Motors' (Fig. 103). The two-piece chocolate block at the top is the recipient of the two coloured cables from the switch just referred to. Just to reiterate, if the motor goes in the opposite direction to that we are expecting from the switch position, it is these two cables that need to be swapped round.

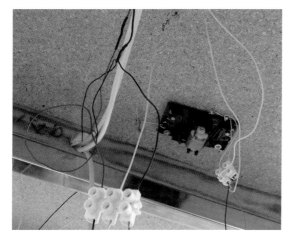

Fig. 159 Fulgurex point motor installed and wired up.

The frog connection is the three-piece chocolate block and the only stipulation is that the centre cable for the frog itself is yellow and the other two cables coming in are our red and black track feeds. If it should be that the frog is swapped over when powered up, by which I mean that the loco runs against a point blade selection instead of with it, change the green and brown cables over.

The green and brown colours used have no significance in themselves, they were just left over after the red and black have been used for feeds, orange and blue for fixed 12V DC and yellow for frogs. That only leaves the white cable out of the eight and that will be used for negative on the LED colour light signals as that is what Berko use.

Figure 159 shows an excursion under the station baseboard and towards the buffer stops. The point motor in view is one of the pair for the crossover. There are two white cables coming from the point motor and terminating in the chocolate block. The white and yellow cables coming in are actually from the other point motor in the pair, as this is a crossover and only has one switch. The cable colours are kept the same as the colours coming out of the control switch on the panel. If both motors operate incorrectly, change the original yellow and white cables coming in from the controller. If only one point motor doesn't operate in the right sense, change the white cables over coming out of that point motor.

Moving to frog operation and we can see the yellow, brown and green cabled chocolate block that we made up in the kit. This has now been joined by a yellow frog connection, which we can see is soldered to the dropper provided by Peco. The point frogs on a crossover are close together and we can see the connection to the other frog in the picture. The last piece of this jigsaw is the two feeds from the track, red and black, which have been taken from a pair of droppers or feeds up the track a bit. Note that the baseboard has been marked with the felt-tipped pen RED and BLACK as a reminder of which rail is which colour, looking towards the buffer stops.

Note the three white cable groups A, B and C coming out of the control panel connector, which in

Fig. 160   Fiddle yard control panel.

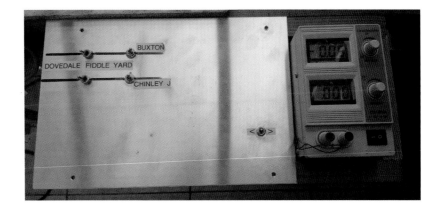

turn mates with the control panel connector itself. The cables haven't all been stripped back yet to reveal the eight cores but are stripped progressively down the layout, as needed. A cup hook relieves the strain on the connector and will be cable-tied as part of the tidying up process at the end.

The relay for the frog changeover is out of sight but is wired exactly as shown in Fig. 103 (Chapter 3 'Point Motors').

The cabling appears to be a rat's nest at the moment and will be joined by signal motor cables and lighting power supplies but will be tidied up with cable ties once we know it all works.

Figure 160 is the fiddle yard control panel as a work in progress and the most significant part of this is that the fiddle yard power is selectable from Dovedale to fiddle yard on both branches. These are the two switches on the left, whilst the two switches on the right are for the two-aspect colour light signals that guard entry to the branches going into the fiddle yard.

You may recall that these colour light signals are interlocked with the Dovedale track power selector, such that it is not possible to select the green aspect on the colour light if the power is not selected to Dovedale first, as it is the Dovedale operator who drives trains in and out of the fiddle yard. Figure 140 gives the circuit that will achieve this function.

It has been necessary to wire the system up this far in order to test the complete working track layout. Only when we know it all works thus far can we turn our attention to ballasting the track.

INITIAL SCENIC WORK – TRACK BALLASTING AND PLATFORMS

Figure 161 shows the desolate wastes of the station end of the layout with working track and points,

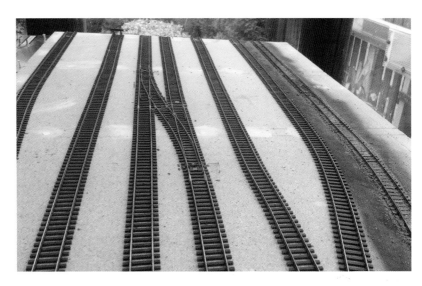

Fig. 161   Ballasting starts with the disused track.

but not much else. When you start scenic work, if the room you have is carpeted, it will need either removing or covering up.

A start on ballasting the track was made initially with the abandoned platform road and the track here did not have the rust colour scraped off the top of the rail surface, as rails here would be rusty and not required to pass current to a locomotive.

Before the ballasting though, apply an undercoat near the track bed of matt black (use the same can as for painting the sleepers originally – see Fig. 31 in Chapter 2 'Track and Point Issues'). This time though we need to use a piece of A4 or foolscap card to prevent spray ending up on the rail surface. This will form the basis of the kind of gunky trackside where the result of about 150 years of oil, grease, and coal and ash ballast have made a kind of black paste near heavily used railway lines. Clean ballast will usually be present though and some vegetation.

The track ballast supplied in bags is usually fairly large stones and it is common for O gauge modellers to use OO gauge ballast. OO gauge ballast can be minimized or reduced in size by two methods: either a kitchen sieve or a Krups' coffee mill. The kitchen sieve will weed out the half-brick sized pieces but for fine work, the coffee mill is the thing. As Krups say in their instructions, the longer you press the button, the finer the grind, so a few seconds are all

that is necessary or you end up with dust. Come to think of it, dust would be useful if you were modelling track tamper machines, autoballasters and the like. The ballast was bought as a job lot from eBay with a load of other scenic materials and was £11; but if you are buying it separately, always go for the fine stuff.

The basic ballasting tools are shown in Fig. 162 and they are:

- Any flat piece of card or cut up nail-file, as shown, to scrape the ballast and heap it against the sleepers after you have applied some in between the track. Make sure you get the ballast in between the track web and rail, which is the bit that attaches the sleepers to one another. This is done with a finger but watch out for any remaining track pins. Make sure point tie-bars are kept free of ballast.
- Polyvinyl acetate (PVA) adhesive dropped in from the bottle with a fine cut across the plastic spout. This arrives as the consistency of Greek-style yoghurt or double-whipped cream and needs watering down to the consistency of milk and the appearance of it. Everyone says you have to add washing-up liquid or any kind of liquid soap to lessen surface tension and improve the flow, so we can go with the flow on that one. Apply this

Fig. 162 The ballasting tools.

sparingly and wait for it to flow on its own and darken the ballast chips. Too much and you will wash the ballast away. Keep the adhesive away from point tie-bars, wherever possible. The rail head will inevitably be glued up but this can be removed with the emery board.

- A tissue or elephant toilet (kitchen) roll to mop up too much PVA leaking out.
- Another piece of emery board or nail-file to wipe over the rails when the PVA is dry.
- A tie-wrap or cable-tie to ferret out ballast from underneath and around point tie-bars and between point blades.

This is always a messy business and there will have to be ballast removed from sleeper tops and the side of rails. Point motors that are in hollowed-out sections of the baseboard can be infuriating victims of loose ballast but we have avoided that possibility.

The Dyson cleaner or similar can then be wheeled out to remove loose ballast, which will inevitably find its way into hitherto working equipment.

Once the track surface has been cleaned off and point motor tie-bars seen to move under power, we can try a train over the finished ballasted track. Not just any train, but consisting of the lightest vehicles, and they must be pulled and pushed over the entire track. What will not derail a heavy class 66 might derail an empty MBA box wagon and it is the ballast stuck to the inside of rail that is a likely candidate. Check-rails at points and crossings need cleaning out with a thin, flat-bladed screwdriver.

When trains run with absolute reliability we can tidy up the track's appearance:

1. Remove track pins and recover for future use. Any that can't be got out, can be treated with a dab of black felt-tipped pen or matt black paint.
2. Clean up fishplates, and solder to rails on either side, using flux and multicore solder. The track breaks needed near points and crossovers provide expansion gaps for ambient temperature changes.
3. Wash fishplates with white spirit and a small paintbrush, then paint with rust track colour.
4. Paint point actuating rods and droppers with rust track colour.

Figure 163 is the runnable track situation after ballasting but there still needs to be ballast picked out and removed from some locations. However, this need not impede progress to carry on the scenic work.

Figure 164 is looking the other way towards Buxton and Chinley Junction and the double-slip has been treated with much finer ballast so as to bed down more easily and not cause any problems with larger ballast chunks – more time in the Krups' coffee mill.

Fig. 163 Ballast in mostly the right places.

Fig. 164 Repeat point operation to keep them clear.

Figure 165 shows a work in progress of the first structures of any kind, which are the Skaledale platforms (£27 for six from Hatton's). It was decided to use these for speed but there is some work to do to get them to look reasonably accurate. Hatton's strategy is to offer competitive prices with exemplary customer service.

The shorter far platform is the rump of one of the platforms that was abandoned in the 1970s of this originally four-platform station. The larger, nearer platform is the two-platform service platform that remains and can just accommodate a 2-car class 158 DMU.

The treatment is as follows:

1. Mark with a pencil across opposite corners diagonally to find the centre. Then drill a 1.5mm hole carefully through the centre of each

Fig. 165 Skaledale platforms in place.

Fig. 166   Workington Station, Cumbria.

platform surface. This will not be the final hole size as the lights will be larger, but it is a pilot.

2. Place the platforms on a perfectly flat surface and even up any inconsistencies in height with coarse-grade sandpaper.

3. Secure the platforms to the baseboard with UHU, which gives you time to move them around before it sets, and run a train past them too.

4. Cover up the gaps between platforms with David's Isopon (£3.75 from eBay) or similar car body filler. This is a two-part mix – be careful not to add too much hardener otherwise it'll set in about five minutes. Also, cut off the locating pegs at the far ends of the platforms with the Dremel-type machine and fill with Isopon. There are no ramps as the platforms are cut down from their original configuration.

5. Sand down the Isopon with coarse-grade sandpaper.

6. Mask off the sides with a sheet of A4 paper and spray from the top only, with Halfords' grey primer (£7.95), which is a pretty good colour match for the original colouring. This gets rid of the rather toy-like appearance of the massively thick, white stripe on the platform, as bought.

7. Restore the white platform edge on the service platforms only with white lining tape (from eBay – 3mm wide, 50m long £7.95). Figure 166 shows us the 2-car length white stripe on the platforms at Workington Station, whilst the rest of the disused platforms are unmarked. Note that the bay platform on the right is white-lined as this is the stabling point for the DMUs. Workington is fortunate to retain its station buildings but Dovedale doesn't have the space, so will need to have a greenhouse-type bus shelter.

We will need to revisit the platforms later to install the lighting and add the shelter, name boards and other details.

MORE SCENIC WORK – DISUSED PLATFORM AND CONTOURS

Figure 167 shows the extension to the disused platform that will be representative of a platform that

Fig. 167 Disused platform and PC box innards.

has had its paving slabs and masonry removed but the original earth works remain. This is constructed from expanded polystyrene recycled from packing boxes (actually desktop PC boxes in this case). This is cut and shaped with a padsaw and jigsaw blade or a 12in (305mm) frame hacksaw blade that has one end bound with tape so that you can hold it safely. This is a really messy business and the Dyson will need to be wheeled out again. The expanded polystyrene blocks, as shaped, are then held down with PVA adhesive, this time in Greek-style yoghurt format.

After the glue has set overnight, you can then contour the terrain some more with the hacksaw blade.

Fig. 168 Modroc plaster bandage on top.

Fig. 169   Carve out a mountain.

The platform is ready to accept the lamps and other details (Fig. 168). The lining tape has backing and fronting tapes. Cut a length of tape approximately to size. Remove the backing tape to reveal the sticky side of the white line. Apply it to the platform edge so that the white line follows the edge. With the Swann Morton scalpel, carefully lift the fronting tape at one end and pull gently and remove the top film. Trim to fit at the ends, also with the Swann Morton scalpel.

The disused platform has been covered with plaster bandage or Modroc (eBay £7.20) to smooth the surface. It just needs a covering with powder exterior grade filler (B&Q £7 per kg) that is mixed up with water to a sloppy custard consistency. If it is any denser than that it may dry as you are applying it. You can also spray the surface of the area to be filled with a water spray, to improve the plaster's adhesion. Flash Bathroom power sprays make good water sprays after they have been rinsed out thoroughly.

Meanwhile, at the tunnel end, there is a tunnel in the making (Fig. 169). The Peco tunnel mouth is offered up as it must fit after the bandage and plaster have been applied; any disparities will be filled in with filler or bush-type scenery. The padsaw is in the foreground with a jigsaw blade fitted but could equally be a hacksaw blade.

Fig. 170   Contour that mountain.

Fig. 171   Real scenery, Edale, Derbyshire.

Fig. 172   Matt black paint and scatter.

Fig. 173   Garden moss on the hoof.

Compare the untreated lunar landscape on the far side with the plaster-bandaged near side (Fig. 170). Note how the far side shows the extra levelled ground of the original track formation when Dovedale had four platforms.

Whilst we cannot hope to replicate the grandeur of the Peak District on a narrow baseboard, this is where we are hoping to capture some of the elements of the scene (Fig. 171). The picture shows Edale in Derbyshire and the line descending to Cowburn Tunnel at over 2 miles (3.2km) long and beyond that to Chinley Junction. The line to Peak Forest and Buxton leaves the main Manchester to Sheffield line at the junction. Please see Fig. 120 (Chapter 4 'Traffic Flows') for the detail on this part of the line.

Whilst there is plenty of scenic work to do yet, the basic contours are in place and a selection of scatter materials applied (Fig. 172); these will form a foundation on which layers of grasses and shrubbery will be built up. The filler-applied surface was painted matt black and scatter materials applied whilst the paint was still wet. It doesn't matter too much what the colour is as long as it is dark; it is all to be covered. A piece of paper with scatter on is offered up to the non-horizontal surfaces and blown into position.

Figure 173 shows the basic raw material for undergrowth and trackside vegetation on the hoof, as it were. It is common or garden (well actually garden in this case) moss that will grow on almost any flat and damp surface outside. It dries to a brown-green colour and resembles the undergrowth of shrubbery near a railway line when all the bits of twigs and other foreign matter is removed.

Figure 174 shows the tunnel area with scenery partially complete and, on the right, is the teased-out and dried-out garden moss secured with milky PVA. On the left is the same base material only this time a layer of teased-out carpet felt (piece on eBay about £5 for a life-changing amount) to simulate taller grasses is laid over the top of the

Fig. 174   Garden moss as scenery.

moss. It is then sprayed with a flexible spray adhesive called Asda Firm Hold Hairspray (£0.70 pence) and then darker green scatter blown on straight after spraying. The dark green was an attempt to simulate hawthorns and similar hedge-type plants that grow on the lineside in profusion. I was not entirely happy with this so some lighter coloured scatter was sprinkled on after another dose of the hairspray.

> ### WARNING!
> Most sprays contain butane gas, which burns at about 1,970°C, as a propellant, so smoking or any other kind of naked light is definitely to be avoided.

Fig. 175   Peco tunnel mouth former of card.

Fig. 176   The tunnel mouth is secured in place whilst the PVA sets.

When using any kind of sprays now it is an idea to use a piece of A4 or foolscap card to mask off the track, as we will not be requiring our trains to stop involuntarily to admire the new scenic bits.

The track still has the marks left by the plaster-type filler used on the top layer of the expanded polystyrene, but as there are limestone trains shuttling in and out of Dovedale, some of the white powdery stuff will remain.

The Peco double-tunnel mouth (£4.50 Hatton's) consists of a light shell moulding (Fig. 175). To beef it up a bit, draw round the 'stone' part of the tunnel mouth onto card with a felt-tipped pen and cut out the shape, making sure you cut inside the line so it will fit. Glue into position with the PVA Greek-style

yoghurt glue. The very edges need to be slightly flexible, as they will need to match up to the tunnel rock face, as modelled.

The wing walls used as retaining walls on the tunnel mouth were not used. They are not always used on the prototype.

Figure 176 depicts a flat piece of scrap wood holding the tunnel mouth in position, whilst the PVA sets. The piece of rough-sawn left over from the baseboards is jammed in position to a sleeper. After the glue has set, the tunnel mouth will be 'plumbed in' to the rock face with teased felt and scatter.

The area at the end of the abandoned platform needs remodelling a bit to accommodate a small yard, where the signal box will be (Fig. 177). It will also be a repository for track materials, which is a common feature all over the network, particularly as the signaller would provide some degree of security for the rails against scrap-metals thieves.

The Bachmann signal box (£7.99 post-paid from eBay) is in position after the base has been remodelled with the same exterior filler we used on the expanded polystyrene (Fig. 178). Note how the signal box is in line with the end of the abandoned platform and reflects an earlier track layout. The embryo stack of sleepers on the track will end up by the signal box.

Figure 179 shows the first work in progress to make the abandoned platform look abandoned. Note there is no white line on the platform edge, for it is no longer in use.

Fig. 177 Excavations for signal box.

BELOW: *Fig. 178 Signal box in pre-1960s position.*

Fig. 179   Used and disused platform contrasts.

The yard is started off with Jarvis cinders ballast (eBay: £2.70 post-paid), although you could use ordinary ballast as that seems to be a recent trend (Fig. 180).

Figure 181 is Llanrwst signal box on the branch from Llandudno Junction to the former slate quarrying capital of Blaenau Festiniog in North Wales, where the class 150 is headed. We can see piles of

Fig. 180   Ash and cinders and sleepers in the yard.

Fig. 181 *Llanrwst signal box in North Wales surrounded by track materials.*

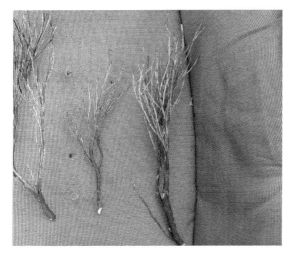

Fig. 182 *Dead heather sprigs for small trees.*

sleepers, ballast and rail outside the signal box. In the white bags at the back near the box are new sleeper keys for the chaired track, just as we have at Dovedale. The goods' shed still survives but all that has been sold off, so the small yard where the box is makes the only practical place for track materials. The abbreviation of S/B for signal box is fairly unusual.

Figure 182 depicts sprigs of dead heather that have been trimmed with scissors to form the basis for small trees. I say small as a layout 2ft wide (610mm) would be dominated by a fully grown model oak tree to the detriment of all else. This is ecologically and environmentally sound when only dead materials are removed from the local moorland, as this stimulates growth in those plants still alive and yet cuts down on materials that would combust readily in response to a carelessly dropped cigarette end or worse.

There are more tree-building components shown in Fig. 183. The Woodland Scenics Foliage appears in a mat form and must be teased out to use economically and realistically. The bits that fall off are as the juices left in the bottom of a roasting pan after a joint of meat has been cooked and must be similarly saved and treasured.

The dead piece of heather can be cut up for small shrubs and will be used to simulate the small birch saplings found in between the tracks of the abandoned platform, as we saw in Fig. 142 (Chapter 4 'Layout Signalling and Final Track Plan'). However, the saplings on the layout will be in leaf.

Figure 184 shows a larger heather sprig that will be a large shrub. The felt is secured with UHU and the matting separated out to form the foliage canopy is visible on the left. The twig may seem a little tall until it is realized that the scenery will be

Fig. 183 Woodland Scenics matting and heather for small trees.

Fig. 184 Teased felt forms the tree undergrowth and bulk.

Fig. 185   A few trees in action, Dovedale tunnel.

drilled to accept the shrub and held in position with UHU. The first 1–1½in (30–40mm) will therefore be buried.

Figure 185 is a selection of the trees and shrubs around the tunnel mouth and, referring back to Fig. 171, there is still more work to do, but with scenery there is no obvious finish line.

Looking the other way towards Dovedale Station, a Northern Metro Rail class 158 excursion sits in the platform, whilst opposite, the abandoned platform and track slowly disappears under the growth (Fig. 186). You can just see the brass gate-post for the signal box yard on the right. This is the same tube we used for the traverser locking mechanisms.

Fig. 186   Disused platform slowly disappearing in the growth.

Fig. 187   Some yard items placed for dress rehearsal.

At the signal box yard, a vehicle appears (Fig. 187). This kind of Network Rail white van is almost a fixture at some places. The van came from eBay from Oxford Diecast at £7.99 post-paid and the Network Rail logo was downloaded from an image on the internet. Then the image was copied and resized in Microsoft Word (you can use Powerpoint instead) until a sheet of A4 was covered with rows of the image, all different sizes. Images from two of these rows were then selected and cut out and stuck on the van with UHU. I then discovered that Hatton's do a Network Rail van for less money but they were out of stock. In any case, there is something more satisfying in making something yourself. Another row of the images will be needed for the Network Rail signs at the depot entrance.

The stacks of sleepers are just sleepers from Peco track that were painted up but not used on the actual track layout. After the webs have been cut off with the Swan Morton scalpel, they resemble actual sleepers, although they are not deep enough in reality. Plastic-based and other kit tracks all have sleepers that are too thin, but this is to enable you to lay track without the need for a massive ballast pile as in real life. Most modellers could not get the Network Rail ballast hoppers through their front door. They are a base of three sleepers laid parallel and succeeding layers laid at right angles to form a matrix that could be handled by a fork-lift truck or wagon-mounted crane.

The rail is from the same track source but, because the rail cannot be painted where the chairs are, when part of the track, when it is dismantled there are gaps where the rust colour did not go that have to be touched in. The rail is mostly cut to 9½in (240mm) lengths, which is a scale 60ft (18.29m) and is a typical length for rail that could be loaded on the older track-laying vehicles and before the widespread use of CWR. As we've seen at Llanrwst and Thetford, CWR is not everywhere and low-speed branch lines would not support a business case for wholesale replacement of older track.

The Peco platelayer's hut at £2.20 has to be a bargain but will need the chimney cut off before it

Fig. 188   Tunnel appears to be a black hole.

can masquerade as a lamp hut. Some areas, up until 2013, were still using paraffin lamps for semaphore signal lighting and the lamp hut was a store for the paraffin and where the refilling and wick-trimming took place. Most of these huts were replaced by Health and Safety green plastic modules, but the original lamp huts survive in many places.

The signal box yard detail has just been parked there for now until the actual positions are arrived at, whence it will be glued down and plumbed in with grasses and other growths. One consideration is manual point rodding coming out of the box.

The view towards the tunnel mouth, although only about 6in (150mm) long, now looks dark inside (Fig. 188). The darkness is caused by black plastic strips of bin-liner bound at the top with duct tape or masking tape or even Sellotape. It is then pinned above the tunnel mouth and trimmed to length with a pair of scissors until hardly any light shows but the trains can brush it aside easily rather than get tangled up in it. If you cut too much off, just re-pin the assembly down the tunnel face a bit. There should always be some light at the end of a tunnel, provided it is not the headlight of an oncoming train! The tunnel curtain also dusts the roofs of passing trains.

Figure 189 is the view of the platforms with the Peco buffer stops glued in position and with the

Fig. 189   Peco buffer stops, without their steam-age lamps, waiting shelter.

Fig. 190   Ratio signal kit and acetone.

oil-lamp mouldings cut off with the Swan Morton scalpel. There will be proper red lights fabricated when the rest of the lighting is installed, similar to those depicted at Fig. 122 (Chapter 4 'Traffic Flows').

The platform shelters are from Trident Models near Nantwich and were £8 each. Trident Models have an astonishing array of stock of all sorts. The owner is very helpful in finding bits you can't see on display.

The basic scenery is mostly in place but will be added to as the layout progresses. Unfortunately this process is not equipped with a STOP button, but continual reference to the prototype scene helps to decide that enough is enough. The back scene is not offered up at this stage, as there are more processes requiring close access and back scenes can get in the way and suffer collaterally from the other process.

SIGNAL CONSTRUCTION

INTRODUCTION

Always with a budget in mind, the decision was taken to use a Ratio LMS Round Post kit together with MSE (Wizard Models) etched brass arms and they come out at £10.49 and £11.40 post-paid. The LMS Round Post kit will provide four signals, each of which has two arms. Going back to Fig. 141 (Chapter 4 'Layout Signalling and Final Track Plan'), there is a bracket signal at the platform end and a further bracket down the track as the double-slip is approached. Both freight reception roads have a two-armed stacked semaphore for the double-slip junction and finally there is one colour light signal for each destination to either Buxton or Chinley Junction. The Berko colour lights were bought second-hand from eBay for £12.95 post-paid for the pair.

SEMAPHORE SIGNALS

Stacked Signals

The semaphore signals were initially assembled with acetone nail-polish remover (Fig. 190). This is a solvent that can be applied like commercially available products but is a good deal cheaper. If you can decant a small amount into a sealed jar, as shown, it is so much the better, as acetone is highly volatile and will evaporate at room temperature quite quickly. As acetone is a colourless liquid it is also a safe idea to label the container. The container shown is from Wilkins of Tiptree in Essex who manufacture jam and marmalade, and these items appear on hotel dining tables all over the world. As you will have paid for the container, what better way to re-cycle than to put it to good modelling use?

Fig. 191 *Stacked signal with strengthener tube and brass pin.*

As it is a solvent, beware inhaling the fumes, as with most of these chemicals it can result in kidney damage.

Acetone is not an adhesive but a welding agent that should give a very strong joint. However, we need to bolster critical joints with epoxy resin, as they will be stressed with the thousands of operations of the signalling mechanism.

Figure 191 is a picture of a stacked freight sidings' exit signals under way. The bases are stuck with epoxy resin to the posts and a brass tube piece (3.18mm internal diameter) is used as a strengthening outer sleeve. The brass tube is drilled to take a brass lace-maker's pin (£3.95 for 300 post-paid from eBay) before we fit it to the post. This is helped by filing a small flat with a file on the tube's outer surface to enable the hole of 0.65mm to be drilled. The lamp and pivot assembly is just secured with the acetone.

The post is actually a 'doll' or small post often used on bracket signals, but a full-height post is not appropriate here for the following reasons:

• In recent years signal posts have been lowered on Health and Safety grounds to lessen the chance of serious injury if someone falls off; this happened recently in East Anglia. This process can only happen if the driver's view of the signal is not impaired by the lowering.
• As the posts are towards the operator side of the layout, the lower they are, reduces the risk of accidental damage, as they will remain delicate objects.
• A high structure, as we saw with the trees, simply emphasizes the narrowness of the baseboards.

The plastic bearing on the lamp moulding will be adequate in view of the small forces involved at the arm. We could cut a small piece of brass tube and epoxy it on, but that would add to the construction time and costs. What will not do is the operating loop on a plastic signal arm, as that will give way relatively quickly.

The black plastic base has been drilled 1.0mm to accept a panel pin to secure it to the baseboard.

Fig. 192   Stacked signals with epoxy resin bases.

The baseboard will be rebated with the chisel to accept the base and then it will be plumbed into the scenery.

Figure 192 depicts both siding exit signals with their brass tube sleeves in place and the small black, angled brackets towards the bottom of the post, secured with epoxy, as it is here the actuating arms will move up and down to transmit movement to the arms. The pin vice on the right is used to open up the holes in the actuating brackets to accept the brass pin.

Figure 193 shows the MSE signal arm with a brass pin soldered to the fulcrum point where the arm will pivot when commanded. This has to be soldered, with plenty of flux, as the arm needs to bounce as per prototype and behind the arm, on the other side of the pivot, will be a backlight cover. This is a shield-type device that moves with the signal arm and obscures the rearward facing light, so that the signaller gets the feedback that the signal has moved

in response to a lever at night, assuming the rear of the signal is facing the signaller.

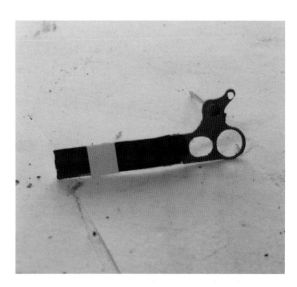

Fig. 193   Wizard MSE signal arm awaiting lenses.

Fig. 194 Lamp and backlight cover detail, Shrewsbury station.

Figure 194 shows the rear of a signal at Shrewsbury. The semi-circular device that looks like a herb chopper is attached to the signal arm pivot. In the ON position shown, a light shines out from the back of the signal towards the camera. As the signal wire is pulled down to move the signal arm to OFF, the herb chopper or backlight cover moves to the right and obscures the light. These backlight covers are usually fitted where the back of the signal is facing the signaller in the signal box, but they can be fitted even if the arm is facing the signaller. The lamp is a converted paraffin lamp and you can see the cable coming out of it, although even paraffin lamps had an electrical connection for a Lamp Out indicator.

MSE do very nice backlight covers in the fret as bought, but these need gluing in position with UHU, as solder would melt the pivot. Superglue would run like crazy into the pivot and the mechanism would never move again.

Fig. 195 Acetate sheet for the lenses.

The arm is dunked in white spirit to remove any flux before painting the front of the signal arm red and the rear white. The spectacle, where the lenses go, is either grey or black. The move in recent years has been towards grey but there are plenty of semaphores around that are still black. The white stripe is a piece from the platform edging reel bought earlier – well, there is 50m of it. This needs the edges trimming with the Swan Morton scalpel. The stripe at the rear is black – simply paint a short piece, say 2in (50mm), with matt black enamel before cutting a piece off and sticking it on.

Figure 195 shows two sheets of coloured acetate sheet, which, together with a yellow sheet, were £2.35 for the three post-paid. These will form the lenses of the signal arms. Blue was historically used as the early paraffin lamps shone yellow and so a blue lens was needed for a green aspect. That lens colour survives today but the paraffin lamps have been replaced by either filament lamp conversions or LED units.

The stationery hole-puncher gives us a basic item to work with from which we can trim the acetate sheet down to size to fit the lens on the signal arm.

Figure 196 shows the completed signal arm with lenses in place. The lenses are secured in place with a tiny spot of superglue, which will quickly run round the aperture and secure the lens in position. The tweezers help to avoid your fingers being spot-welded to the signal arm. The arms have to be fitted to the posts fully finished but the posts may not be fully painted, except for the white post and black attached parts. After it has all be handled in the rigging process to get it to work, the signals will need touching up anyway.

Figure 197 shows a selection of actuating rods, which is the bit that connects the signal motor to the linkages to connect to the signal arm. The plastic ones supplied in the Ratio kit are totally unsuitable and the etched ones supplied by MSE are a bit fiddly and have to be built up or laminated from thin slices to make a substantial piece.

Fig. 196   Complete etched arm – just needs the white tape trimming.

Fig. 197 Signal actuating levers made from code 60 rail.

BELOW: Fig. 198 Stacked signal with actuating arm.

The rods are code 60 rail, which is that used by TT-3 and N gauge track. Hatton's sell a yard (0.93m) of it for £4. The best bit about using rail, which is basically a girder, is that you don't have to mark the centreline with a scribe and steel rule, centre pop and then drill. You can just drill 0.65mm to accept the brass pin and the signal actuating wires. Clean off the drilled holes with a rat-tailed file. The piece of track is ¾in (20mm) long and if it looks as though guess work has been employed as to where the holes have been drilled – that is quite right. Each signal is unique to its situation and so it doesn't matter much as to exact dimensions at this point. The burning question is 'Does it work?'. The distance between the three holes at the one end is fairly important and needs to be about 3–4mm distance between each. On the stacked signals, the last hole will move the actuating wire and the second one in is where the brass pin pivot will be. The third will not be needed and the hole at the far end is where the signal motor attaches.

The rail has to be filed down so that the web of the rail is the same top and bottom and both sides.

Figure 198 is a picture of one of the stacked signals with rigging wire applied from the Ratio kit. The main issue with the rigging wire is that there is a straightened-out Z kink in it to simulate the rod's progress to the arm. The main purpose of this kink is to allow for tuning or adjustment. A loop is made

Fig. 199   Stacked signal in position with panel pins.

that fits round the middle hole in the actuating rod near the bottom of the post. It has a pronounced hook on it and this is necessary at this stage as we do not want the wire to slip off whilst we are trying to line it all up. Create the straightened Z, as referred to in Fig 198, then finally create the hook in the far end of the wire, as near as possible to keeping the arm horizontal when the actuating lever is at rest. Any slight deviation of the arm from the horizontal position can be tweaked by nipping one angle of the Z to be less than 90 degrees if the arm droops, or extending it to be more than 90 degrees if it is higher than the horizontal. There is a further means of tweaking the arm position after installation but this will do to start us off.

In Fig. 199, the rodding shows up more clearly, as it now contrasts matt black with the white of the post. When the wires are painted, just slip a small piece of paper between wire and post to avoid the post ending up with zebra stripes.

Notice the two Z kinks in the rodding and that the arms are more or less horizontal. We have to attach the steel weight of the signal motor (Fig. 106, Chapter 3 'Semaphore Signal Motors') and this may yet change the way the arms sit. Also, if the arms move too quickly, we may wish to attach a crocodile clip to the signal motor steel piece, under the baseboard, and this may also affect the way the arms sit. This is why we need a further adjustment mechanism.

The post has been secured with four panel pins and is rebated into the board, as we don't want the signal base to show up on the finished model. Signal posts are usually sunk into the ground to some depth and do not have a black base as they are usually modelled. Colour light signals, on the other hand, do sometimes have a visible base on which the signal is bolted to a pre-prepared concrete base. The two holes for the signal motor wires are in the foreground and are 1in (25mm) apart. That is the minimum they can be with two motors mounted side by side underneath the baseboard. The actuating arms have been bent to go some way to meet up with the signal motor wires.

Fig. 200   Stacked signal ready for use.

Fig. 201   Stacked signal with travel adjusters.

Figure 200 shows the signal operational from a temporary power supply and before the interlocking is connected in. The two thinner wires coming out of the baseboard at the signal post are the actuating wires from the motor, and the larger, angle-cranked wires are for fine adjustment. An angle-ranked wire that sits beneath the actuating wire is for horizontal arm adjustment and the one above is for signal OFF adjustment.

In Fig. 201, the story is rewound slightly to show the operation of the signal. The upper arm is off and when the motor is de-energized, the actuating arm will fall and rest upon the horizontal arm adjuster on the right of the post. There doesn't need to be an OFF adjuster, as we can see the yellow light behind the blue lens quite clearly. In any case, we can alter the OFF adjustment by the addition of a crocodile clip underneath the motor. The lower arm, on the other hand, has an OFF adjuster where the actuating arm will strike the brass wire adjuster, when it reaches the fully OFF position. The bracket signal is another part of the story and is covered next, but you can see a similar arrangement of adjusters on that signal too. You can add an end-stop to the arm by gluing a piece of brass that stops the arm in either the horizontal or OFF position, but this is not adjustable once it is glued in. Brass tube signals from MSE would be easier to set up in this regard.

The link (https://youtu.be/JArNA_uVXhg) is to YouTube and quickly shows the signal operating. Please excuse the handheld camera, operating the switch and writing this book at the same time, but it should convey how the arm can bounce.

Bracket Signals

Figure 202 shows that the bracket signals are under way. The shorter signal is the platform starter signals and the rationale here is that there had been a platform canopy at Dovedale and the lower bracket signal was preferred for driver sighting reasons. In reality there is only one of each type of signal in the kit, but still remarkable value.

Fig. 202   Bracket signals under construction.

Fig. 203   Bracket signals angle cranks.

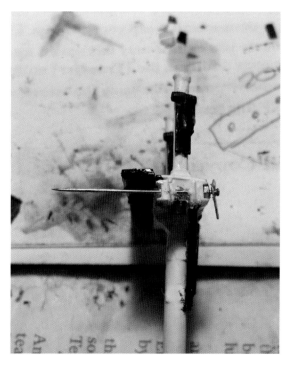

Fig. 204   Bracket signals angle crank securing with brass pin.

Bracket signals need four angle-cranks to transmit the movement from the actuating arm on the post to the signal arm (Fig. 203). Depicted are four of the MSE cranks from the fret as bought and they need to have their etched holes eased out slightly with either a rat-tailed file or the sharp end of a Swan Morton blade to accept the signal wire. Then thread the centre hole onto a brass pin and use a 12 BA nut (£2.65 for ten post-paid from eBay) as a washer on the back. This will make the bracket assembly stand off the girders of the signal bracket so that it can move freely. The crank is left free to rotate and is not glued or soldered to the brass pin.

Figure 204 shows the smaller bracket signal with the crank fitted. The hole drilled with the pin vice is 0.65mm or the diameter of the brass pins you have. There are some areas in the book where no stress has been put on dimensions, as in some cases it does not matter – here it does. The brass pin needs to be an 'interference fit' – in other words, you need to push it in firmly but gently. This means you can tweak the all-important clearance between the crank and the signal bracket. When it is as shown in the figure, apply the epoxy to the gap between the girders and where the pin is showing, and trim off the end of the brass pin.

Figure 205 shows the four cranks in position for the smaller bracket signal. The two cranks for each side must be lined up and connected first, but with reference to how it will work. In Fig. 205, the wire connected to the signal arm must be pulled down for the arm to go OFF. If you follow the links to the second crank near the post, you can see that the crank on the post must go up for the arm to go up. The link between the two cranks must be arranged so that the crank near the post can go up. In the figure you can see that it clearly can. This then drags the signal arm wire down and the arm goes up or

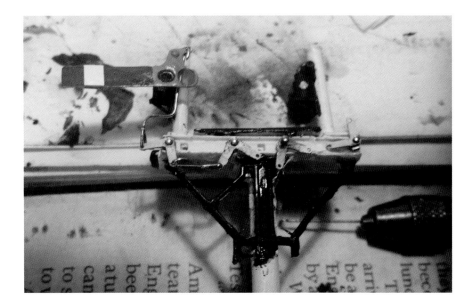

Fig. 205 Bracket signals angle crank linkages.

BELOW: *Fig. 206 Platform end bracket signal ready for use.*

OFF. This also means we must connect the actu-ating lever to the opposite side from the stacked signal in front of the signal post. The Z crank on the wire nearest the signal arm not only gets the wire over to the arm, but is a primary adjuster. Repeat this for the other signal.

Figure 206 shows the platform starter signals ready, operationally, but still with a few details to go on, such as handrails and the track-circuit diamond. Freight lines may or may not be track-circuited, passenger lines invariably are, although this can be sparse as we saw at Scropton Crossing. Figure 125 (Chapter 5 'Absolute Block') shows a yellow piece of track and that is the only track-circuited piece on the layout.

The ladder is from the Ratio plastic kit and would be improved if an etched version were used. Also, an etched one bends if struck, whereas a plastic ladder will snap – but there is a budget. The area has been 'scenicked' with static grass summer mixture straight from the packet. It has a less electrified look that way (Jarvis £1.85 a bag from eBay).

Figure 207 shows the freight-exit stacked signal motors mounted underneath the baseboard. The pair of motors to the left is for the bracket signal for the double-slip from the passenger platforms and the run-round loop. Note the length of steel armature protruding from the motors when they are de-energized. It is enough to provide attraction when energized but not too much where the range of movement would be limited. In other words, if less steel is showing, there will be less movement. More steel showing and the coil may not attract the steel well enough. The amount shown is enough.

The one motor with the crocodile clip attached has been damped or the movement made less fierce. The crocodile clip can also act as a signal arm upper-limit movement end-stop. It may need some UHU as the clip will be progressively pushed down the motor shaft until it falls off otherwise. The snag with this is it is not adjustable once glued. Note that the signal motors are secured with the same no.8 screws we used on the traverser deck cupboard door bolts and point motors.

Fig. 207   Stacked signal motors in position.

Fig. 208   Using a punch to line up signal motor.

If a crocodile clip is not enough to dampen a movement, a piece of solder wrapped round the clip adds weight and is easily trimmed to suit. The short YouTube clip tends to accentuate the rapid movement of the arm, but it is adjustable to taste.

The large red cable coming in from the left with the crocodile clip on the end is the temporary connection to the locomotive controller, so that we can see what voltage and current are necessary to make all this work correctly.

The installation of a motor is under way (Fig. 208). The holes on a pair of signals must be far enough apart to enable two motors to sit side by side with either a bracket or stacked signal; they are 25mm here and 3mm in diameter. We still have to get the motor lined up beneath the hole so that the brass actuating wire does not touch the sides of the baseboard. A dowel or screwdriver, as shown, enables us to locate the motor. Mark one hole with a felt-tipped pen, then use a sharp screwdriver to make a small hole, 3–5mm deep, in the baseboard. Offer up the motor and screw to the baseboard using the pre-prepared hole. The motor may be able to rotate slightly about this one screw and that usually helps in finding the path of least resistance. Insert the steel armature from the bottom and ensure that it is free to move up and down. Apply power and make sure the armature remains in position and attracted by the coil. This position is the maximum height the signal arm will go off when connected to the signal actuating arm. With no power applied, ensure that the armature is in the position roughly where you see it in Fig. 207; this amounts to about 15mm of the armature showing when de-energized. This is the signal arm ON or danger position. Apply a crocodile clip to the actuating wire above baseboard level to stop the armature disappearing onto the floor. Bend the actuating wire to connect with the lever on the post. Bend the end of the wire over so that it cannot come out of the lever hole. A later modification was to ensure that the bent-over last bit of the wire touched the baseboard and acted as

Fig. 209 Signal travel adjusters made using brass wire.

BELOW: Fig. 210 Signal motor under test using loco controller.

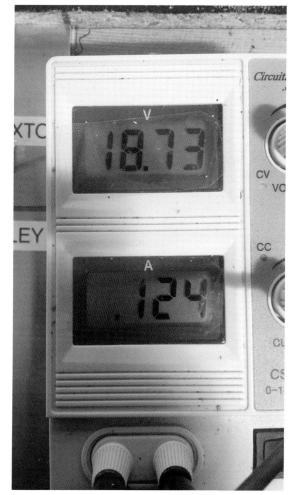

a signal ON end stop. This does mean it is fiddlier to get the wire through the actuating lever hole.

Finally, mark and screw in another no.8 screw, making sure you do not disturb the setup. You may need to back off the original screw slightly to make sure the motor ends up at right angles to the baseboard.

Figure 209 is a somewhat gruesome close-up of the bracket signal in Fig. 208. The thinner brass wires come up from the armatures that move when energized. The thicker wires are end-stops to limit signal arm movement. Note how this time the bracket signal works by moving the signal rods up, whereas the stacked signals work by pulling it down, to pivot the arm up. The signal post is held in position by two panel pins and will be plumbed in when all the adjustments have been made. When this is done, care has to be taken to ensure that no scenic material impedes the mechanism and that it is stuck down properly. As this is such a simple mechanism, it is very reliable. The worst that happens in normal service is that some scenic material gets down one of the holes and jams up the works. Simply remove the two fixing screws from the motor, leaving the armature suspended, and blow through to clear any obstruction. Replace and all will be well. This can happen after the baseboards have been moved. If you neglect to run trains regularly, the odd spider can get down there, although the spider's exit is quicker than the entry when the signal is powered up.

Although the signal motor coils are nominally 12V, it was found that to operate reliably, the voltage had to be increased (Fig. 210). On show is the maximum voltage of the loco controller, with the direction switch set to OFF or we might have a class 66 approaching high Mach numbers. This 18V is perhaps a little high but 12V is not enough for a bracket signal. We can see that the motor takes 0.124A or 124mA. There will only ever be two semaphore signals operated on the layout: the platform bracket and the bracket in Fig. 208. This means a total current of signal motor power of 0.248A or 248mA. A further power supply was acquired giving out 24V and capable of supplying up to 2A (eBay £6.25), and this was adjusted using the 'pot' to be 22V.

The interlocking relays limit the number of signals operable at once and that will remain at 12V operation but now the relay contacts will be passing 22V.

This is not altogether unexpected as we increased the air gap between the armature and coil to give more bounce. This has the side-effect of lowering the magnetic force, so we must increase the voltage to compensate. Electric motor efficiency is partly a function of how small the air gap between stationary and rotating parts can be. The smaller the air gap, the more efficient the motor is, but the more difficult to manufacture it is and, consequently, the more expensive it is. The solenoid is really a linear motor.

The colour light signals remain at 12V and will be covered later.

The signals are short-duration operation and only take current when they are OFF or 'go', so there will be no problem in running the voltage higher than rated and the insulation is well capable of dealing with the voltage.

Work is well under way to install the station throat semaphore signal layout (Fig. 211). Each signal post signals two possible destinations of either Buxton, on the left, or Chinley Junction,

Fig. 211   Station throat signals installed and awaiting some detailing.

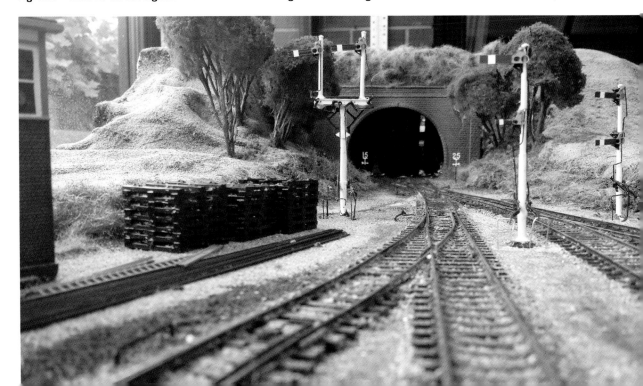

Fig. 212 Skegness Station in Lincolnshire viewed from the carriage sidings.

on the right. This is as opposed to the platform starter bracket signals, which just signal their own platforms. The signal on the right controls the exit from either the right-hand reception siding or the locomotive/cripple wagon siding. This is quite in order, as Fig. 212 shows.

Figure 212 shows the station throat area of Skegness Station in Lincolnshire. The camera is standing on a public walkway that straddles three carriage sidings, which are actually loops. The only signal that controls exit from any of the sidings is the subsidiary armed signal on the left. Note also the points after the main line entry/exit are manually lever operated. The signal on the right is for the down main-line running in to the station and all the other signals with their backs to us are platform

starter signals with subsidiary arms for the carriage sidings. The main line is track-circuited, with the lozenge figure on the post, and the sidings are not.

CONTROL AND INTERLOCKING

Once we have the eight semaphore signals installed and working from the loco power supply, thoughts turn to wiring the signals up to the control panel using the newly acquired 24V power supply. Inserted between the control switches and the signals must be the interlocking panel, which has to be fabricated after the principles laid down in Fig. 139 (Chapter 4 'Signal Interlocking'). There are a total of six cables in the figure and this is only for one signal, so the interlocking panel will be busy as there are eight semaphore signals altogether. The colour light signals have their own interlocking panel in the fiddle yard because they are interlocked with the fiddle yard section switches.

Figure 213 is a variation on the printed circuit board (pcb) that we used for the traverser deck locking mechanism, except that this has holes drilled into it to accept electronic components. The pcb is sold as Vero or prototyping board, where a boffin devises a circuit by trial and error and then sends the working version off to be turned into a repeatable production version. This means that we must change the circuit to suit what we need. The boards were £2.50 for two from eBay.

Mounted on the board is one of the relays we looked at in Figs 99 and 100 (Chapter 3 'Point Motors'). The two pins sticking out of the board on the top-right are the coil, and the circuit has been broken between the coil using the twist drill and pin-vice, as shown in Fig. 213. If we look down the board to where the contacts are, we can see that the board has been arranged to avoid a short-circuit

between the pins, quite by chance as it happens but less work for us. When you buy a board like this it is a bit of a lottery, but you can usually find the path of least work. What you do then is connect one of the coil connections to the outer piece of pcb and that will be the negative for the 12V that will operate the coil. Solder the pins using a wipe of flux and the multicore solder, and one relay is ready. Repeat that for the other seven relays. On the same figure is a row of 1N4001 diodes from the bandolier of 100 we bought earlier. There were thought to be thirteen combinations of point position that have to be interlocked with the semaphore signals. In the end, only twelve were used; as is often the case, an interlock in one position affects an interlock elsewhere. For example, with a platform bracket signal there are two interlock positions: the platform point and the point out onto the run-round loop. However, the other bracket signal uses the same interlock for the second point, as that point must be in the same position for both signals (see Fig. 141, Chapter 4 'Layout Signalling and Final Track Plan'). After that

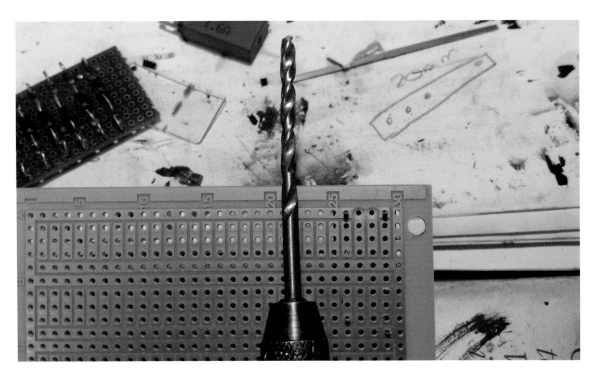

Fig. 213   Using a drill to insulate pcb strips or circuits.

Fig. 214   *Interlocking relay panel and diode circuit boards.*

the other bracket signal comes into play and is separately interlocked.

In real life, passenger-carrying lines that have track circuits are also interlocked with points and signals and block instruments, but this would be a connection too far on the model.

Figure 214 shows the relay panel with the eight signal relays fitted. Signal A is the platform bracket, B is the double-slip bracket, C is the reception starter and D is the outer reception and loco/cripple wagon siding starter. '1' is always towards the far edge of the baseboard and '2' nearest the operator and, in the case of stacked signals, '1' is Buxton and '2' is Chinley Junction. Figure 141 layout plan (Chapter 4 'Layout Signalling and Final Track Plan') refers to signal lettering and their positions. The smaller circuit board with the diodes leads to the relay coils from the point motor switches and it is this connection that provides the interlock by switching any signal relay for which the path is not correctly set. So, even if signals are not being used, the relay operation can be heard when points are

changed. It is only if signals are selected that the circuitry comes into play.

Note the smaller 24V signal power supply fitted next to its larger current-capacity 12V version and both are mounted so as not to foul any switch or control panel-mounted equipment.

Figure 215 shows the pre-wired module made up on the bench before fitting to the control panel.

CAUTION!

Not all power supplies arrive with a terminal cover and where this is so, remove the mains power socket and bind the terminal block with white electrical insulating tape (eBay £0.99). Should you subsequently require access to the terminal block, remember to remove the mains plug from the socket before starting work.

The coil negative supplies run round the outside and its blue cable can be seen going from top-left to bottom-right and this is 12V.

Each signal supply is represented by a single colour coming in from the signal motor switch on the control panel and then going out to the baseboard, this is 22V. This wire is connected across the normally closed contacts of the relay. The positive of the relay coil is connected to the point motors that, if changed to a conflicting route, will operate the relay and lock the signal power out for that signal. There are two examples of the signal supply in clear view: two white and two yellow cables on the middle-left. The white cable bundle marked AAA is the outgoing cable to the connector on the left and the baseboards. Yellow is signal 1D and white is signal 2D. You don't have to mount the relays on the pcb, it is just tidier this way. The same convention to wiring has been retained, as shown in the table.

Wiring convention

Pin	Wire Colour	Signal
1	Red	1A
2	Black	2A
3	Orange	1B
4	Blue	2B
5	Brown	1C
6	Green	2C
7	Yellow	1D
8	White	2D

Connected around the sides of the pcb are the 12V supplies from the point motor switches on the control panel, through a diode that will interrupt the signal supply if the point is incorrectly set for a given path. The usual way of determining which of the two-point motor supply wires is used is by trial and error. First, set the point to conflict with the signal indication and when the relay operates

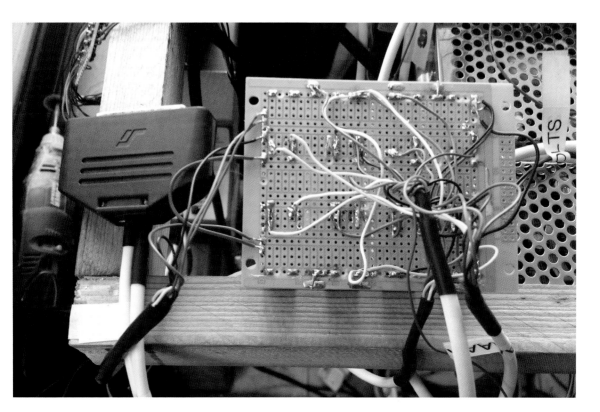

Fig. 215   Rear of interlocking panel showing point motor feeds to operate lockout relays.

and the signal returns to danger, that is the correct point motor switch wire connection. Then return the point to be in line with the signal indication and the signal should be able to be pulled OFF or go.

Colour Light Signals

Some of what follows here is also relevant to the next section 'Lighting'.

LEDs typically used in railway signals and other railway applications operate on a voltage of 3V or less. In order that they should work with a 12V supply, it is necessary to drop the difference across a resistor. If you apply 12V across an LED its life will be bright but short.

The two colour light signals were acquired second-hand from a private sale on eBay. Consequently, they were about half the usual store price (£12.95 post-paid). Interestingly, though, both red LEDs were inoperative and this prompted thoughts, apart from a partial refund, about the current flow in those LEDs and what made them pack up. The items were repaired easily enough.

The light head is a plastic moulding but the rectangular back plate is just stuck on with adhesive. Just ease the Swan Morton blade in there carefully and it will come off. There is one piece of wire running vertically up the lamp head for the white or negative, which is common to both LEDs. The LEDs have the legs cut off and a red cable soldered to the positive of the red LED and green cable for the green LED. Test a new LED on the loco power unit with the long lead as positive and no more than 3V. Trim leads but keep an eye on which is which or mark the negative with black felt-tipped pen on the side.

The assembly lifts out but be careful not to draw the red, green and white wires too far up the lamp post or you may not get them back again. Solder a new red LED in place – it is always the lower of the two lamps in a colour light signal, as that position is best in the driver's eye line. If you get the polarity wrong it will not light up at all, so give it a test using the loco power supply before you re-assemble. (Fifty of the red 3mm LEDs are £1.49 post-paid on eBay, but measure the diameter before

you order.) Re-assemble the light unit and replace the rear cover and secure with either a drop of acetone or UHU. Paint the rear of the head matt black.

Figure 216 is a picture of the repaired red LED in operation and the significant detail here is that the lamp is only taking about 9mA or 0.009A. The usual tariff, current wise, is about 20mA, but anything that is under-run from its rated value will last longer and, perhaps, with tolerances in manufacture, 20mA is slightly too high and that accounts for the reason both red LEDs were expired on purchase. The light

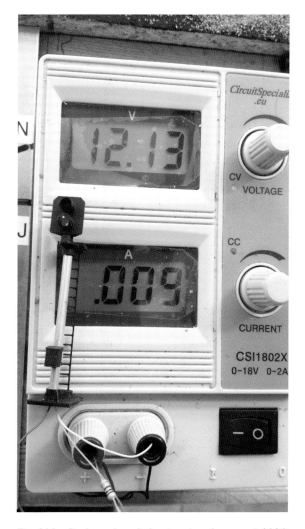

Fig. 216 Berko colour light signal under test, 1,000Ω resistor.

output is satisfactory, as the signals, as modelled, are not the high-intensity LED types to be found on Network Rail. Current in a circuit can be reduced by the insertion of a resistor and they are measured using the symbol Ω, which is the capital Greek letter omega. The actual unit is called an ohm after the physicist who figured it all out.

The value often used is 470Ω or 470ohm and resistors come in what is known as preferred values, although whose preference they are has been lost in the mists of time. If we increase the value to 1,000Ω or 1kΩ that will roughly halve the current flow.

The red LED in Fig. 216 has a 1kΩ resistor fitted. If you find you only have 470Ω, and you can measure this with the meter, then add another 470Ω resistor after the first one, in series. With different makes of LED, it is possible that the 470Ω resistor value is the correct one, but if the LED seems very bright, then 470Ω is too low. A bandolier of fifty 470Ω resistors is £1.98 post-paid from eBay. If you are in the slightly unlikely situation where the LED is not bright enough, you can wire another resistor of the same value in parallel or across the original one and this will bring the resistance down to half the value of one of the resistors. Weird I know, but this can be proved mathematically (if you are at a loose end one weekend). Once we have installed these colour lights, we shall not wish to uproot them any time soon to change the LEDs.

Figure 217 is an ultra-bright LED signal at Annan in Dumfries and Galloway on the Carlisle–Dumfries–Glasgow line. If your ordinary colour light signal is this bright it needs another resistor – it is not going to last at that rate.

Fig. 217   Ultra-bright LED signal at Annan Station, Dumfries and Galloway.

Fig. 218   Usual brightness colour light signals, Llandudno Junction Station, North Wales.

Fig. 219   Berko green LED under test.

Figure 218 is the more usual intensity red colour light signal at Llandudno Junction in North Wales. The Virgin Voyager is bound for Bangor and Holyhead.

There are moves to change over Network Rail from the low- to high-intensity LED colour light signals but the question is how far will they get with this before lineside signals are done away with?

Figure 219 show the green aspect and that takes considerably less current at 6mA, showing that the characteristics of these LEDs can be different when using the same resistor value. If you have LEDs on the same signal whose characteristics are different, then you have to tune them with differing values of resistor inserted in the green and red cable paths. If they are the same, just use the white negative or return cable.

The signals need to have their bases drilled with a 1.5mm drill before mounting on the layout. In addition, as their placement is right by the tunnel mouth

Fig. 220   Berko colour light signals installed at Dovedale tunnel mouth.

and baseboard join, the cables had to be run in the tunnel mouth to a drilled hole where the signal wires can meet up with the wiring underneath the fiddle yard baseboard. The bases are secured with the two nails each from the co-axial cable clips we acquired earlier. These nails are meant to drive into walls and brickwork, if need be, have sharp points and a head that you can get a punch onto to gently hammer in.

Figure 220 shows the colour light signals in position but not 'scenicked' in until there has been a bit of operating and what electronics boffins like to call the 'burn in' period. In other words, kit like this is more likely to go phut early on. This is why

extended warranties and the like on electronic consumer goods are of such questionable value. If it lasts a year it'll probably do ten years. The steam-age speed-restriction signs have been updated with the Network Rail arrows advising drivers which track the sign refers to. The etched signs are £7.95 from Trident Models near Nantwich. This is a model shop where you can rummage to find the bits you weren't quite sure you needed but are convinced you do when you see it. You can cut the letters out with the Swan Morton scalpel.

As we are now entering a TCB area there are no lozenges on the signal posts, as it is all track-circuited.

Fig. 221 Class 158 signalled for Buxton.

Fig. 222 Class 66 signalled for Chinley Junction.

Figure 221 shows a class 158 on its way to Buxton. The platform 1 bracket is OFF, as is the left-hand Buxton junction. After the double-slip it is the Buxton line; all completely interlocked so that the train will be going there with the signals that are set and the station controller will be driving it all the way. This must be a special, as it is usually the class 153 that does the Buxton trip.

A Freightliner class 66 has the OFF to return limestone empties towards Chinley Junction but will travel only as far as Peak Forest South and the quarries there (Fig. 222).

LIGHTING

INTRODUCTION

Figure 221 shows that the layout is being progressively enhanced in the scenery department as the infrastructure installation such as signalling permits, and this process continues in tandem with the next piece of construction.

The lighting section is to do with lighting effects that will enhance the layout and the use of lighting for indication. If the layout is to be subsequently used at exhibitions, then some means of external mains lighting would be needed to illuminate the layout as a whole for the paying public, but we are not concerning ourselves with that here.

DAY/NIGHT ILLUMINATION

The layout lighting is split up into two sections, mainly for reasons of control in that the day/night stuff will need to be switchable but the operational lighting is also separately switchable. The operational lighting will be on, any time a train is running; whereas the other lighting will be in use in low-light conditions.

Day/night illumination consists of platform lighting and yard lighting for freight operations. These lamps were acquired from eBay for £4.48 for four post-paid. The lamps consist of two fine copper tubes that fit inside one another and a lamp head fashioned from brass. The lamp base is a plastic moulding. Fine wiring runs up inside the tubes to the ultra-small LED. They need ballast resistors to throttle back the voltage so that we can use 12V straight from the power supply. However, for just over a pound each they are good value. There are floodlight towers for freight yards but these are too tall for the narrow boards and would impede operations.

Figure 223 shows a lamp under test and the resistor is nominally 1,000Ω or 1kΩ. This is easily arrived at by two of the 470Ω resistors in series or connected one after the other, which is nominally 1,000Ω. In the example shown, it is actually a 1kΩ example but no matter. The resistors supplied are 470Ω but the LEDs are too bright – street lights do

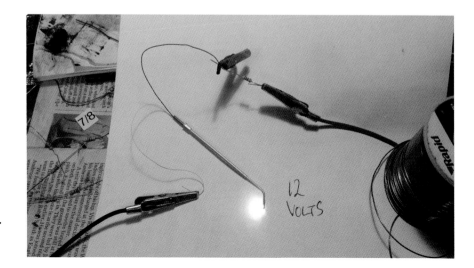

Fig. 223   Platform or yard lamp under test with 1,000Ω resistor.

not usually come with xenon technology. Note that, somewhat unusually, the red positive cable of the 12V supply is connected to the black fine wire and the negative to the white fine wire to get it to work.

Figure 224 shows an assembled lamp with resistors – this time two 470Ω examples in series. You can just see their outline under the black heat shrink tubing that shields the resistor and lamp connection. The other white positive lamp cable has had a red cable soldered on to present red and black underneath the baseboard. The original holes drilled on the platform now need opening out with a 3mm drill so that we can pass the cables, one by one, through the platform face and underneath the baseboards.

OPERATIONAL ILLUMINATION

This consists of the buffer-stop warning lights we saw at Buxton in Fig. 122 (Chapter 4 'Traffic Flows'). There seems to be much variation as to their construction, placement and use on Network Rail, so some scope exists for the model to appear in any of these guises.

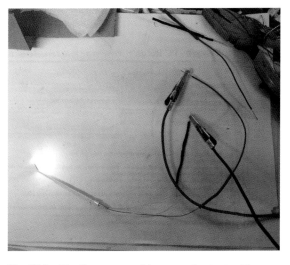

Fig. 224 Platform or yard lamp under test with 1,000Ω resistor and ready to fit.

Figure 225 is a case in point at Llandudno Station in North Wales, where the buffer-stop warning lights seem to be an adapted traffic lamp of the type used on road cones. Note the bullhead railed and keyed trackwork.

Fig. 225 Buffer stop lamps at Llandudno Station, North Wales.

Fig. 226   Buffer stop lamp with brass tube and 1.8mm LED.

Figure 226 shows the basic building blocks of the buffer-stop warning lamps. The 3mm tube is a remnant from the traverser loco siding locking device and we need two of these at 2¾in (70mm) length. The lamps will be 30mm apart to provide a driver eye-line light at different ranges from the buffer stop. The lamps themselves are 1.8mm red LEDs, although these items look orange they shine red (eBay pack of ten, £1.64 post-paid). Two slots are cut into the tube with the square rat-tail file illustrated at the top of the picture.

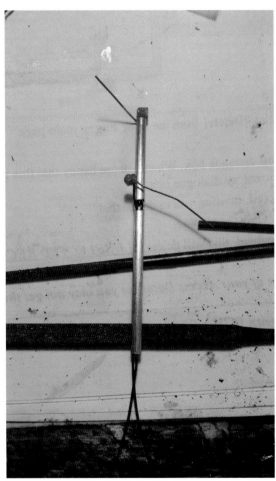

Fig. 228   1.8mm LEDs slotting into position.

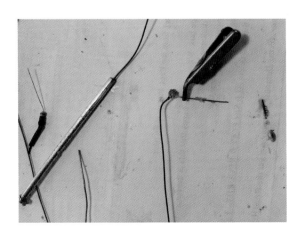

Fig. 227   1.8mm LED with epoxy on positive and tinning the negative.

Figure 227 shows that the longer positive lead has been cut back and a red cable soldered to the stump. The crocodile clip is used to conduct excess heat away before tinning the negative lead. This negative lead will be soldered to the brass tube after trimming. The positive connection has been coated in epoxy resin adhesive to avoid a short-circuit with the tube.

Figure 228 shows both LEDs threaded through their slots and the red leads appearing from the bottom. When the negatives are trimmed and soldered to the tube, it is this soldering that will hold the LEDs in position; but they can still be fine-tuned to point in the right way.

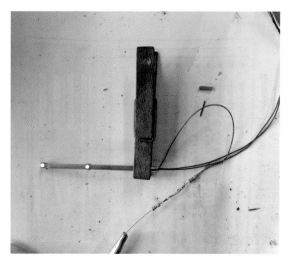

Fig. 229 Buffer stop lamps under test with 2 × 470Ω resistors.

Figure 229 shows the completed assembly under test with 12V. The green lead is soldered to the tube and there are two ¼W 470Ω resistors in the line between the green cable and supply. The resistors were insulated from that around them by heat-shrink tubing. The completed units were brush-painted silver.

The completed assemblies were wired in using cable group C on the baseboard to control panel connector and were connected via a control panel switch to the 12V 4A supply terminal block.

Figure 230 shows a view of the completed buffer-stop warning lights in use. The station building is from a photograph of Cromford Station on the Derby to Matlock line. This building has survived but is not in railway use now.

Fig. 230 Buffer stop lamps operational.

The fencing is war-gamer Jarvis, £2.99 for 6ft (1.85m) and the framing is wire-mesh garden netting from Poundworld cut up with the tin shears and sprayed with Halfords' grey primer. A tree is needed for the corner, and the platform and yard lamps need securing in position after testing in situ.

Figure 231 is another view of the passenger facilities at Dovedale but with platform lights and red warning lights in operation. The class 158 has the road and is ready to depart from the Buxton platform.

Fig. 231   Class 158 departs with buffer stop lamps and platform and yard lamps operational.

CHAPTER SIX

SEQUENCE AND BLOCK BELLS

INTRODUCTION

Network Rail refers to a working sequence as a working timetable (WTT), which includes all scheduled train or locomotive movements, and is the output on the signal box Trust computer on Network Rail. This is as opposed to what is on Trainline.com, which is a passenger timetable.

Figure 232 shows the Trust computer, NEC multisync monitor, at Brough East signal box with the WTT displayed and a running commentary of what is happening to the trains.

We are not concerned with running to a timetable, as time cannot be adapted to a 1:76 scale and, in any case, we would have long periods with no movement, which is hardly the point of operating the railway. This is all the more important if you are running at exhibitions, where the paying public expects, and has a right, to see trains moving nearly all the time.

In the sequence there must be every movement that would take place, as every movement must be sequenced to ensure there are no embarrassing situations where a train arrives at an already occupied siding and suchlike un-railway-like goings on. In addition, we know the make-up or consist of our trains and where they will fit in the sidings loop and fiddle yard. There will not be much scope for altering the consist for those reasons. Network Rail find similar problems and whilst a class 59 could haul a 3,500 tonne train from the Merehead Quarries in Somerset, it would not fit into the Pewsey goods' loop, nor probably its eventual destination, without shunting.

The block bells are the last plank in the operational ship and are needed for station and fiddle yard operators to communicate, as on Network Rail.

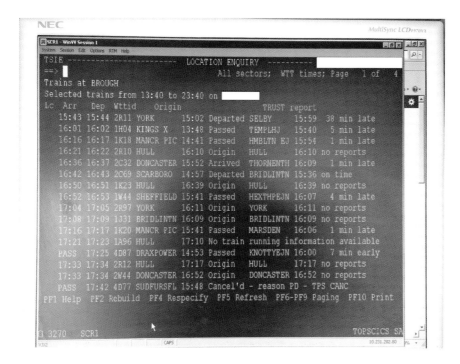

Fig. 232 Trust computer display at Brough East signal box, East Yorkshire.

THE SEQUENCE

The planning simply uses Fig. 141 printed out and a set of brass pins with each separate possible train movement identified by its own labelled pin.

Figure 233 is just such a setup with the all-important piece of corrugated cardboard underneath. This performs the crucial dual function of being able to retain a pin that has been stuck in and avoiding the desk looking like it has woodworm.

The passenger pins are on the left and are:

- Class 158 DMU 2-car Northern Rail Metro for the excursion (158 NRMetro).
- Class 158 DMU 2-car Northern Rail for the Chinley Junction and Sheffield timetabled services (158 NorthR).
- Class 153 DMU single-car for the Buxton Shuttle (153).

The freight and light-engine pins are on the right and are:

- Loaded Limestone 1 (LS1).
- Loaded Limestone 2 (LS2).
- Limestone Empties (LSE).
- Light Engine (LENG).

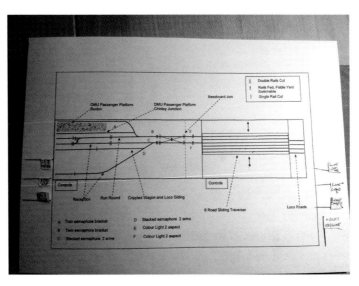

Fig. 233 Fig. 141 printed out with brass pins for train identifiers.

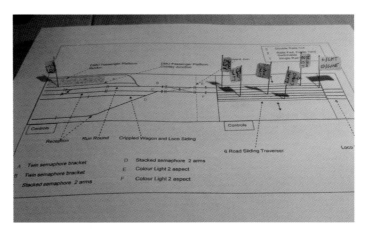

Fig. 234 Dovedale sequence under construction.

The day's starting point must be determined and the sequence must end up with all the stock in the right positions ready to start a new day. In addition, we need one fiddle yard road vacant at all times to enable freight locos to run round their trains.

Figure 234 shows the rolling stock in its starting positions at the beginning of the sequence. The class 153 is not in its rightful platform, as it is only the Chinley platform that has the hosepipe stabling facilities. This means that the DMU must swap platforms before setting off, as the automated train describer on the platform will only be able to cope

with a Buxton train arriving and departing from the Buxton platform. Similarly, when the day is almost done, it will arrive at the Buxton platform and then stable at the Chinley platform overnight. This must be referred to in the sequence notes and is exactly the sort of thing they do at Buxton now.

The two class 158s, 158NorthR and 158NRMetro, are one behind the other in the fiddle yard, as the excursion is not due to arrive at Dovedale until mid-morning. You may recall we put in a section break on the first two roads on the fiddle yard for this very reason.

The light freight engine is an early candidate to stable in the loco siding at Dovedale, as it is taking up half a fiddle yard road. It could be stabled on one of the loco roads at the end of the fiddle yard but would need to be got out of there at some point. In any case, it is needed to back onto a train at one point.

All three limestone trains occupy a road each. Clearly if we stabled the empties in the Dovedale yard overnight, that would free up another fiddle yard road for the Lafarge cement hopper train that was mooted in the planning stage. However, for now we have the trains that will work the branches. This means that there has to be one freight in the station yard at all times to keep the fiddle yard clear to operate.

The compilation of the sequence took about an hour because once you have the basic configuration set up, it is just a matter of copying lines in Word or whichever word processor you have; the Notes column may vary though. The sequence compiled is in Appendix II, towards the end of the book. There are thirty-four station and fiddle yard moves and a further two moves relating to the stabling of the class 153 single-diesel unit. The limestone trains have to either be run round or have a loco to release, and the differing colours enables the fiddle yard operator to make these manoeuvres easier by planning ahead and seeing what is coming up.

It is important:

• Not to make the sequence repetitive or predictable, as this makes it tedious for both operators and spectators; you can engineer in variations, although not too many. An example of this is the arrival of an empty limestone train when there is already a loaded one in the looped reception road. This also makes use of the light engine.
• The stock all has to end up ready to start another sequence and as a sequence would take around forty minutes to an hour, exhibition use will see about five or six complete sequences. The customers don't seem to mind that night follows day and so forth, as long as something moves.

• With the freights, balance is reasonably important; you can't really have more loaded than empty trains, as one place would end up with most of the wagons in real life. Although most exhibition customers wouldn't notice, some who stand there watching the entire sequence will. The fact there is only one empty train and two loaded just keeps the pressure off fiddle yard space.
• The sequence should fit on a page of A4 paper pinned to a board, and a crocodile clip is used to keep up with where both operators are.

I daresay there is a 'phone app or desktop computer program to achieve this, but by the time you have input the variables and learned how to use it you could have done it this way and then gone to the pub to discuss it with friends.

BLOCK BELLS

The principle of the block bell is based on the old-fashioned electric doorbell, except that with an electric doorbell, when the button is pressed and the bell energized, it breaks the circuit to the solenoid coil of the bell, thus returning the bell to where it started. If the button remains pressed, it then re-energizes and rings again, de-energizes again and just keeps ringing as long as the button is pressed. Here we do not need the 'interrupter' contact, just a single button press will produce a single beat on the bell.

Electric doorbells, which we could have used, have now achieved retro status and are consequently out of budget range on the market, so we have to make our own – although B&Q do a traditional-type doorbell for £9. However, this would need to be modified to bypass the interrupter contact.

Figure 235 shows a schematic block diagram of the block bell wiring or, perhaps more properly, the bells should be labelled as train describers. A single press on the button produces one ring of the bell. 12V was used, although there should not be any problem in using the 24V signal supply if required,

Fig. 235 Block bell construction and operation diagram.

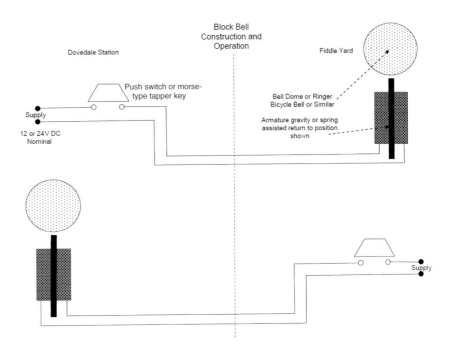

BELOW: *Fig. 236 Fiddle yard train describer bell.*

as the action of the bell is momentary and, although we are using 12V relays, that rating is continuous. As the block bell system is not polarity-dependent, we can use yellow and white from the fiddle yard B cable group connector for the bell signal from Dovedale and brown and green for the fiddle yard bell signal to ring the bell at Dovedale.

Figure 236 shows the fiddle yard block bell. The driver is a 12V solenoid left over from another project but was £2 post-paid from Hong Kong and eBay. It looks like a device for actuating a valve in an air-conditioning system or similar. The rest of the assembly was from the scrap box. The only item of note is the brass wire holding the bell clapper loosely in position. As the solenoid armature could rotate, we don't want it rotating out of the line of the bell dome.

Figure 237 shows the fiddle yard backboard, which is an old 1990s pine small table top. This performs three functions:

1.   Buffer stops for the loco roads in the fiddle yard.
2.   Block bell above baseboard mounting position.
3.   Sequence holder.

The block bell is wired to run through the fiddle yard deck along with the loco supply cables and to emerge at cable group B. From there it goes into the control panel and out again on the inter-board connector on cable group B again. We can trace the yellow and white wiring easily, onto the Dovedale board and through to the control panel there again on cable group B. As all the connectors were pre-wired and tested, this connect-

Fig. 237 *Fiddle yard backboard with train describer bell and sequence holder.*

Fig. 238 *Fiddle yard sequence holder in operation.*

ing up is quite simple and achieved quickly. Most connectors were wired with all the connections, even though they are not actually used at present. A 'tail' of about 1ft (305mm) was connected in to those connections not needed immediately. This is just easier than unpicking it all to wire in extra connections at some later date.

The block bell at Dovedale, operated from the fiddle yard, is similar in construction but the bell dome must not sound quite the same. A circular tin makes a reasonable bell dome.

The sequence holder is a piece of A4 card that has been 'stood off' the backboard by two strips of ½in × ¼in (12mm × 6mm) stripwood (£1 for this much) and secured by panel pins. This positioning is to enable a crocodile clip to act as a pointer and be moved.

Figure 238 shows the sequence mounted on the piece of A4 card and secured with a crocodile clip. This sequence has been laminated for durability and will withstand coffee spillages. Laminating machines are available for a little as £10 and supermarkets sell the laminating sheets quite cheaply.

Figure 239 shows the pushbutton for the block bell (£0.99 each from eBay post-paid) at the fiddle

yard. It would have been quite nice to have a morse tapper key but they are also highly prized collector's items now that morse is no longer in use, and so would bust the budget.

The button has to be ergonomically near the controller direction switch, as that is where an operator's hand will naturally be a lot of the time.

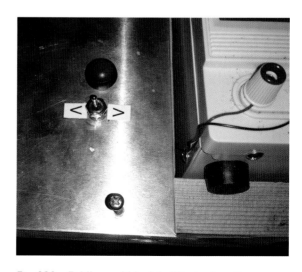

Fig. 239 *Fiddle yard block bell/train describer push in position, fiddle yard control panel.*

CHAPTER SEVEN

CLOSED-CIRCUIT TELEVISION (CCTV)

INTRODUCTION

Network Rail and the train-operating companies have been using CCTV for years. NR uses them for crossing supervision, tail lamp cameras and security. The TOCs use CCTV for security.

In a model context, CCTV is almost always used to remotely observe and control trains that are not in the direct sight of an operator. This does not apply to Dovedale in its present form but is used where there are hidden or concealed tracks, or if the railway operates in separate buildings or outdoors.

CCTV ELEMENTS

Figure 240 depicts a diagrammatic representation of a small CCTV system of two cameras feeding one switchable monitor. The monitor is of the type used in cars for a DVD player but has an additional switching feed to select a second camera.

This is popularly used to connect to the reverse gear switch in the car's gearbox so that the view is automatically switched to a rearward facing camera when reverse gear is selected. We shall not be using this automatic switching but we will be using the manual switching facility. The views on the monitor are referred to as V1 and V2 on the monitor front panel. Some versions of monitor, including the one depicted, come with a remote control.

Cameras and monitors are usually manufactured using the RCA Phono system of connector, but the most readily available and adaptable form of wiring between camera and monitor is the BNC co-axial system. The cabling resembles terrestrial TV and satellite aerial cable. Phono cables extend to about 16½ft (5m), which is not usually going to be far enough. BNC cables are available up to 164ft (50m). Much longer distances may lead to signal loss.

It is necessary to buy adapters to convert from Phono to BNC but these are about £0.50 each and

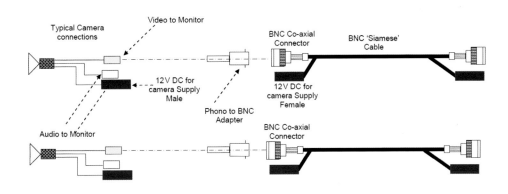

Fig. 240
Diagram of two
CCTV cameras
and one monitor
for a small system.

readily available from eBay. The BNC cables used are termed 'Siamese' in that they have a 12V power cable integral in their construction. This is necessary otherwise you would have to supply each camera separately with 12V. The BNC Siamese cables are available on eBay from £3 upwards, depending on length. The 12V power supply would be another of the 12V 4A units that we purchased earlier for point and relay operation.

The monitors range from £13.99 to about £25.99 for versions ranging from 4.1in (10cm) to 7in (18cm) display. They are easily mountable for an operator to view. The larger monitor has a diagram on the listing of how you connect it up: the red and black leads are for the 12V power supply and blue is for the reversing switch feature, so is unused in our application.

Figure 241 shows a miniature CCTV camera that also has a microphone, although that feature is not used and the Siamese cables referred to earlier do not support audio. The cameras are £2.99 each plus £2.70 air mail from an eBay seller in Hong Kong. Once again, allow two weeks for the package to sit in customs. They cannot be mounted directly outside but must be sheltered from the worst of rain, snow and ice, just like the railway. It is astonish-

Fig. 242   Colour CCTV camera mounted in position.

ing that the camera has a manual lens focus ring for optimum image quality.

Figure 242 shows one of the cameras mounted looking down towards the fiddle yard storage sidings on the O gauge model railway that runs between three sheds in my garden. The sidings are outside of the shed that contains the fiddle yard and whilst it is fine to have the shed door open in summer, that inclination declines when it is −5°C (23°F) outside. Note that the audio cable is not connected as the white Siamese cable has only video and 12V DC connections.

Figure 243 shows the view from the camera in Fig. 242. High-quality HDMI it is not, but there is enough information to help fiddle yard operators manage trains to place them in the right order for

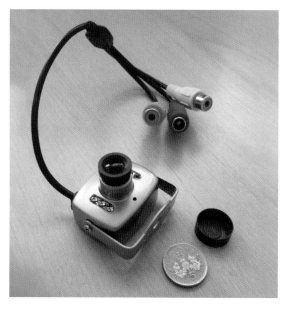
Fig. 241   Colour CCTV camera.

Fig. 243   The view from the mounted CCTV camera.

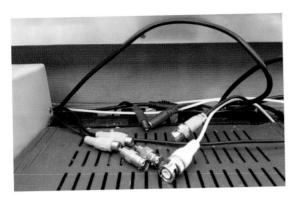

Fig. 244　Set of two CCTV camera connections to one monitor.

Fig. 245　Argos small TV to show more signal detail.

the sequence. The sidings are 16ft (4.88m) long and the silvery object above the tracks in the picture is another camera completing the sidings' surveillance system.

Note the switching of video from V1 to V2 on the control panel.

Figure 244 shows the fiddle yard now with the camera connections undone so we can see how it connects. The two yellow sockets on the left are the inputs to the monitor. Just to the right of those sockets are two Phono to BNC adapters, and after that is the white and black cabled BNC cables and connectors. There is only the black Siamese-cabled 12V DC connector coloured red in the picture, but not visible is another for the white-coloured BNC cable. It doesn't really matter which way round the cameras are connected to the monitor unless you have a definite preference for a particular camera to be V1 and the other to be V2. The black DIN connector in the background is the link between monitor and power supply.

Figure 245 depicts an Argos 14in (35.6cm) television at £50 as the monitor to show more detail of signals at a junction. The right-hand track is signalled to go to the left-hand branch at the junction that is coming up beyond camera shot. This junction is outside the sheds but must be viewed by all three operators. Two operators need to exchange trains and one needs to know what the others are up to. The fiddle yard operator is about 70ft (21.3m) from the camera.

The only criteria of the TV are that it has:

- Wall-mounting bracket screw inserts on the rear.
- Phono video output.

When you set up the TV you select either EXT or AV Video, meaning the TV is to use the phono socket as an input.

Figure 246 depicts two BNC T-pieces that enable us to feed the video output from a camera to the monitors of more than one operator. The type shown has two female and one male on the same T-piece. The more usual configuration is three females, so that BNC cables can be connected to all three. The tariff on eBay for a three-female T-piece is £1.59 post-paid. You can also use the T-pieces to join two lengths of BNC cable.

Fig. 246　BNC T-piece connectors.

CHAPTER EIGHT

DOVEDALE SUMMARY

To round off the book, here are a few views of the layout at the stage where the book ends. It is tempting to say the layout is finished but there is much small detail work and more scenery to go yet.

Figure 247 depicts class 153 railcar stabled at platform 1 at Dovedale Station and one of the first sequence moves is to platform 2 for a Buxton departure and, similarly, at the end, the reverse is true.

The class 153 is signalled for its departure from platform 2 at Dovedale Station (Fig. 248).

A class 66 when it arrives can have no coupler on one end to preserve the front skirt (Fig. 249). The black-painted brass wire allows us to retain the skirt but still couple up. The silver paint on the buffer shanks enhances realism. The limestone load is ballast chippings with cement dust added and a little water.

TOP LEFT: **Fig. 247   Class 153 stabled in platform 1 at Dovedale Station.**

BELOW LEFT: **Fig. 248   Buffer stop overview of class 153 departure.**

BELOW RIGHT: **Fig. 249   Class 66 arrives with loaded limestone train.**

Figure 250 – it's all go at Dovedale. Or, more correctly, the only one going is the class 158 to Sheffield via Chinley Junction. More cement dust on the wagon sides makes them look as though they have been to a quarry.

Figure 251 shows a 24/7 Dovedale with a DB Schenker class 66 arriving with a Limestone 2 train in the gathering gloom.

The point rodding is a work in progress (Fig. 252). Note the groups of two rods heading off to the double-slip and platform throat point, as all these have facing point locks, as well as a rod for the tie-bar. The former lamp hut still has the Health and Safety warnings, although all signal lamps are electric now. Working signal lamps in 4mm are possible, but not by me.

ABOVE: **Fig. 250 Class 158 departs for Sheffield.**

Fig. 251 Class 66 arrives with loaded limestone for Buxton and Manchester.

Fig. 252 Dovedale signal box and point rodding.

Figure 253 shows the signal box yard layout and there needs to be a ramp over the point rodding coming out of the box. The equipment cabinets are the polythene covers from the ends of an HDMI cable sprayed with Halfords' grey primer. The signage is printed Dymo 450 address labels cut up and applied using their self-adhesive backing. The end nameplate is one of the station ones and they were done with an aluminium drinks can cut up with good scissors to simulate an aluminium plate. The Network Rail Hungarian border fencing is a scale 10ft high (3m), but its height is obscured by the disused platform.

The signal box has only eleven rods coming out of it now compared with around twenty-five in steam days. The single rod on the left is for the crossover.

Fig. 253 Dovedale signal box yard.

The freight yard still has the old coal merchant's hut hanging on (Fig. 254). The EWS branded monster box is a cripple and has had the front coupling removed to avoid the class 57 inadvertently coupling up to it.

The spare rail has been dumped here, as there is no more room at the signal box yard.

Class 153 is on its way on another Buxton shuttle out of platform 2 (Fig. 255).

Fig. 254 Dovedale freight yard.

BELOW: *Fig. 255 Dovedale Station throat with a Buxton departure.*

ABOVE: **Fig. 256** *Fiddle yard ready to start a sequence.*

Fig. 257 *Fiddle yard, and Buxton has the track.*

The fiddle yard is ready to begin operating with the class 153 first to appear to take up position in the platform 1 stabling area (Fig. 256). All stock is kept in the fiddle yard when not in use and the cover is in the background. The cut up compost sack hides the fiddle yard from Dovedale.

Figure 257 shows the fiddle yard exit roads, where far is Buxton and near is Chinley Junction.

Only one lines up at once to keep down the stress factor and each road is individually selectable for either Dovedale or fiddle yard by the fiddle yard operator, and the colour light signals are interlocked with these selections.

Figure 258 is an overview of a class 153 departure for Buxton with the class 57 waiting for move number 18 on the sequence.

Fig. 258   Dovedale Station overview from the tunnel-mouth top.

LAYOUT COSTINGS

Costings are based on purchases from April to September 2015. Although the costs of some tools are mentioned in the text, they are not included here nor are any rolling stock or locomotives featured on the layout. The listing is in the order in which they appear in the text and this fits in with the construction order. The CCTV section has not been totalled up as no CCTV was used on Dovedale and so only indicative costings have been included.

Minor items such as a squeeze of washing up liquid to make the track ballasting go better have been omitted, but this has to be balanced by the fact that some items come in larger quantities than actually used.

Baseboard construction – B&Q

Item Description	Quantity	Cost Each – 2015 £	Sub-Total (£)
1,828 × 610mm × 12mm chipboard	2	£11.08	£22.16
1,800 × 38 × 25mm rough-sawn timber	Pack of 8 timbers × 2	£8.00	£16.00
Drywall 40mm countersunk Philips-head screws	Pack of 1,000 in box, 1 box	£7.00	£7.00
Traverser Deck – 8mm outdoor ply 1,220 × 1,220 mm	1	£20.00	£20.00
Note: one pack of the rough-sawn timber was returned			
Total cost for this section			**£65.16**

Track – all from Hatton's, Smithdown Road, Liverpool

Item Description	Quantity	Cost Each – 2015 £	Sub-Total (£)
Peco SL-100F Code 75 railed track	1 pack of 25 yards	£64.00	£64.00
Peco rail built buffer stops	5	£1.40	£7.00
Peco double-slip SL-E190	1	£35.00	£35.00
Peco SL-E195 Medium point RH	3	£33.00	£33.00
Peco SL-E196 Medium point LH	3	£33.00	£33.00
Peco Fishplates	4	£2.20	£8.80
Total cost for this section			**£180.80**

See text for suppliers from here on.

Further baseboard, track and fiddle yard construction

Item Description	Quantity	Cost Each – 2015(£)	Sub-Total (£)
Red Dog baseboard joiners	1 pair	£5	£5.00
Set of four legs	1 set	£90.00	£90.00
Halfords' Matt Black spray paint	1	£7.99	£7.99
Protective eye-wear	1	£1.50	£1.50
Plywood for traverser deck	1	£20.00	£20.00
Aluminium angle, traverser	1	£10.00	£10.00
no. 8 ½in (12mm) screws	Bag of 25	£2.00	£2.00
Baseboard screw holes filler	1 Box	£1.50	£1.50
Decking screws, 75mm	Bag of 25	£2.00	£2.00
SMP sleepers OO gauge	Bag of 100	£6.50	£6.50
Brass wire 24 AWG	15m	£2.50	£2.50
Copper-clad sheet, traverser locking	1 sheet	£2.99	£2.99
Brass tube – 3.18mm	300mm length	£2.38	£2.38
Brass rod – 1.2mm	300mm length	£0.89	£0.89
Total cost for this section			**£153.25**

Electrical equipment

Item Description	Quantity	Cost each – 2015 (£)	Sub-Total (£)
Micro-switches	Bag of 10	£2.50	£2.50
12V DC fixed power supply	1	£6.95	£6.95
18V DC 2A stabilized power supply (loco control)	2	£47.33	£94.66
Electrical test meter	1	£3.20	£3.20
Mains cable	2m length	£4.99	£4.99
Mains plug	1	£1.50	£1.50
Diode	Bandolier of 100	£1.69	£1.69
Relays	Job lot of 50	£9.80	£9.80
25-Way D-type connectors	Pair male/female	£2.00	£8.00
25-Way D-Type shrouds/covers	Pair	£2.00	£8.00
Eight-core cable	100m drum	£24.36	£24.36
Heat-shrink tubing	1 pack	£5.00	£5.00
24V 2A power supply – signals	1	£6.25	£6.25
Total cost for this section			**£176.90**

Further layout construction and scenery materials

Item Description	Quantity	Cost each – 2015 (£)	Sub-Total (£)
Coach bolts, power supply fixing	Bag of 10	£2.50	£2.50
Control panel aluminium plates	Pack of 2	£6.50	£6.50
Crocodile clips	Pack of 10	£1.80	£1.80
White coaxial cable clips	Box of 100	£1.79	£1.79
Scenic materials – job lot	1 box	£11.00	£11.00
Skaledale platforms – job lot	Set of 6	£27.00	£27.00
Coarse-grade sandpaper	Pack of 10 sheets	£1.00	£1.00
UHU impact adhesive	2 tubes	£1.00	£2.00
David's Isopon	1 double-tube set	£3.95	£3.95
Halfords' grey primer car paint	1 tin	£7.99	£7.99
Lining tape 3mm × 50m	Reel	£7.95	£7.95
B&Q Exterior-grade filler	1kg	£7.00	£7.00
Modroc plaster bandage	2 packs	£3.60	£7.20
Carpet felt	1 piece	£5.00	£5.00
ASDA firm hold hairspray	1 tin	£0.70	£0.70
Peco 00 double tunnel mouth	1	£4.50	£4.50
Bachmann signal box	1	£7.99	£7.99
Jarvis cinders ballast	1 bag	£2.70	£2.70
Oxford diecast transit van	1	£7.99	£7.99
Peco platelayer's huts	2	£2.20	£4.40
Static grass summer Jarvis	1	£1.85	£1.85
Etched signs – speed	1 pack	£7.95	£7.95
Street lamps – 4	2 packs	£4.48	£8.96
1.8mm red LEDs	10	£1.64	£1.64
Fencing war-gamer Jarvis	2 packs	£2.99	£5.98
Wire netting intended for garden	1 roll	£1.00	£1.00
Epoxy resin adhesive	1 pack	£1.00	£1.00
Superglue	8 tubes	£1.00	£1.00
Hardboard for backscene – cut	4 pieces	£7.99	£7.99
Art Printers 00 backscene – dales	1 roll	£12.94	£12.94
Wills' point rodding kit	1	£11.50	£11.50
Wills' point rodding extension kit	1	£9.25	£9.25
Bachmann passengers	2	£6.95	£13.90
Total cost for this section			**£194.23**

Signal construction

Item Description	Quantity	Cost each – 2015 (£)	Sub-Total (£)
Ratio LMS round post kit	1	£10.49	£10.49
MSE Wizard etched signal arms	1	£11.40	£11.40
Berko colour lights	2	£12.95	£12.95
Brass pin lace-maker's pin	300	£3.95	£3.95
Coloured acetate sheet	2	£2.35	£2.35
Code 60 rail	1 yard (0.93m)	£4.00	£4.00
12 BA nuts	1 pack of 10	£2.65	£2.65
Pcb Vero board	2	£2.50	£2.50
50 red LEDs	1 pack	£1.49	£1.49
Bandolier 470Ω resistors	50	£1.98	£1.98
Total cost for this section			**£53.76**

Block bells and sequence

Item Description	Quantity	Cost each – 2015 (£)	Sub-Total (£)
Solenoids 12V	2	£2	£4
12mm × 6mm stripwood	600mm	£2	£2
Pushbutton for the block bell	2	£0.99	£1.98
Total cost for this section			**£7.98**

Total cost for the complete layout: **£832.08**

CCTV

Item Description	Quantity	Cost each – 2015 (£)	Sub-Total (£)
Phono to BNC adapter	each	£0.99	£0.99
BNC Siamese cable	5m length	£3.00	£3.00
Monitor 7in	each	£25.99	£25.99
Camera	each	£5.68	£5.68
Argos 14in TV	each	£50	£50
3-way female T-piece BNC	each	£1.59	£1.59

OPERATIONAL SEQUENCE

Dovedale working sequence, September 2015

No	Origin	Branch	Bell	Description	Notes
1	DD		-	153	From stabling to Buxton platform
2	FY	CJ	3.1	158NorthR	To Chinley platform, ex-Sheffield
3	FY	CJ	2.3	LENG	Class 57 to Cripple/Loco
4	DD	BX	3.1	153	Store in front of Class 158 Metro
5	FY	CJ	5	LS1	Freightliner run-round reception
6	FY	BX	3.1	153	To Buxton platform
7	DD	CJ	3.1	158NorthR	Back two roads in FY
8	DD	BX	3.1	153	Not in front of Metro
9	FY	CJ	4	158NRMetro	Metro Excursion to Chinley platform
10	DD	BX	5	LS1	Freightliner Front four roads
11	FY	BX	4.1	LSE	Run-round Reception
12	DD	CJ	4.1	LSE	To Peak Forest CEMEX works
13	FY	CJ	5	LS2	DB Schenker run-round reception
14	FY	BX	3.1	153	To Buxton platform
15	DD	CJ	2.2.1	158NRMetro	Empty stock for service Manchester
16	FY	CJ	3.1	158NorthR	To Chinley platform
17	DD	BX	5	LS2	DB Schenker front four roads in FY
18	FY	BX	4.1	LSE	Reception siding, isolate. Class 57 to back on
19	DD	BX	3.1	153	Back two roads in FY in front of Metro
20	FY	CJ	5	LS1	Freightliner run-round reception
21	DD	CJ	4.1	LSE	LENG to cripple/loco siding after release
22	FY	BX	3.1	153	To Buxton platform
23	DD	CJ	3.1	158NorthR	Ex-Chinley platform for Sheffield
24	DD	BX	5	LS1	Freightliner front four roads
25	FY	BX	4.1	LSE	Run-round reception
26	FY	CJ	2.2.1	158NRMetro	Empty stock returning excursion, Chinley platform
27	DD	CJ	4	158NRMetro	Metro excursion return Manchester
28	DD	BX	3.1	153	Back two roads in front of Metro

Dovedale working sequence, September 2015 *(continued)*

No	Origin	Branch	Bell	Description	Notes
29	DD	CJ	4.1	LSE	
30	FY	CJ	5	LS2	DB Schenker run-round reception
31	DD	BX	5	LS2	DB Schenker front four roads in FY
32	FY	BX	4.1	LSE	Run-round reception
33	DD	CJ	4.1	LSE	
34	DD	CJ	2.3	LENG	To stable at Peak Forest overnight
35	FY	BX	3.1	153	To Buxton platform
36	DD	-	-	153	To stable in Chinley platform overnight

Legend

LS	Loaded Limestone 1 is Freightliner, 2 is DB Schenker loco-hauled
LSE	Limestone Empties Freightliner Class 66 or 57 loco-hauled
DD	Dovedale Station
FY	Fiddle Yard – everywhere else
BX	Buxton branch
CJ	Chinley Junction branch
153	Class 153 Northern Rail Single-Car Unit
LENG	Light Engine
158NorthR	Class 158 Northern Rail 2-Car DMU for Sheffield service
158NRMetro	Class 158 Northern Rail Metro 2-Car DMU used on excursion

INDEX